2 v. set 900p
T
k-65

THE UNITED STATES OF AMERICA

OF AMERICA

A Syllabus of American Studies

THE UNITED STATES OF AMERICA

A Syllabus of American Studies

Volume Two: History and Social Sciences

by

ARTHUR P. DUDDEN, PH.D.
Bryn Mawr College
Bryn Mawr, Pennsylvania, U.S.A.

PHILADELPHIA
University of Pennsylvania Press

CMenSP

7413
Printed in the United States of America

Introduction

This *Syllabus of American Studies* was prepared to help both students and teachers obtain a broader and deeper understanding of North American literature, language, arts, history and social sciences. It does this by identifying and directing attention to the most significant aspects of these fields and by pointing out profitable lines for additional inquiry. It is written to assist those persons who desire to obtain a better understanding of life and culture in the United States. At the same time, it is written in terms broad enough to challenge both university students and individuals not enrolled in formal academic programs.

The *Syllabus* is based directly on the books required for reading for the University of Pennsylvania examination for the Certificate in American Studies. But it does not attempt to parallel or condense the American civilization curriculum of the University. Instead the *Syllabus* is intended to have broad usefulness and to serve both as a basic guide for formal instruction at foreign universities or other educational institutions and also as a guide to the reader engaged in individual study. Inquiry concerning the University of Pennsylvania Certificate should be made at the Cultural Office of the United States Embassy or Consulate and *not* directly to the University of Pennsylvania.

This *Syllabus* is designed to provide a topical organization by pointing out major aspects to which attention should be directed, to guide and stimulate inquiry, to arouse curiosity, to point out interrelationships and thereby increase understanding. It does not in any way take the place of the books themselves or the reading of them; it does not provide a condensation of the books; and it does not supply easy answers to possible examination questions.

The *Syllabus* is published in two volumes. Volume I deals with North American literature, language and the arts, and

Volume II with North American history and the social sciences. Each section of the *Syllabus* follows closely the arrangement of the required readings, and the contents are based directly on these readings.

Each section is divided into five parts:

I. *Required Readings* identifies the books from the reading lists which pertain to each topic.

II. *Major Topics* provides an outline to show the important factors and sub-factors of each topic which will aid the student to understand the topic and broaden his comprehension of the required readings. These outlines provide mere starting points for substantial understanding. Thus they direct attention to points of inquiry, and the required readings indicate where the information can be found.

III. *Discussion Problems* present problems of the kind which demand a sustained probing beneath their surface aspects, and thus they require considerable effort before full understanding can be achieved. They are intended to be difficult as well as provocative, in order to draw out the student as much as possible. The value of these questions will depend on whether only a brief answer is attempted or one involving considerable additional study and research.

IV. *Study Exercises* vary in form from one topic to another because they are designed to fit the contents of each topic and to stimulate understanding and expression. These exercises can aid materially in constructing meaningful bridges for comparing life in the United States with human experiences elsewhere. Thereby they can help to increase understanding and good will among the peoples of the earth.

V. *Additional Readings* supplement the lists of required books to show sources for additional information.

This *Syllabus* was prepared with the needs of both students and teachers in mind. It is hoped it will serve its purposes well. The study of life in the United States of America can be absorbing; teaching students about America can be rewarding as well as challenging. The rest is up to you. Good Luck!

ARTHUR P. DUDDEN

Contents

Part A: Geography and History

The Land and Its Resources

I. REQUIRED READINGS
   G. F. Deasy, P. R. Griess, E. W. Miller, and E. C. Case, *The World's Nations*, pp. 18-193, 908-911.

II. MAJOR TOPICS: The Land and Its Resources

A. *The general problem for students*
   1. To understand the natural conditions of life in the U.S.A., and to recognize those natural phenomena which help to shape and direct the patterns of American living
   2. To make illustrative comparisons between the U.S.A. and other regions of the world

B. The United States of America (U.S.A.)
   1. Continental dimensions and relationships
      a. Ranges of latitude and longitude
      b. Between the Atlantic Ocean and the Pacific Ocean
      c. Canada to North
      d. Mexico, West Indies, and Gulf of Mexico to South and Southeast
      e. Soviet Union across Bering Straits
   2. Separated Portions
      a. Alaska
      b. Hawaiian Islands

C. Coastal regions and waterways
   1. Atlantic seaboard
      a. Rivers and harbors of major significance
      b. Sheltered coastal waterways and canals
   2. Gulf Coast
      a. Florida and the Keys

3

      b. Estuary of the Mississippi River
      c. Other areas of maritime importance
   3. Pacific Coast
      a. San Francisco's advantages
      b. Puget Sound
      c. Other areas of maritime importance
   4. The Great Lakes
      a. Major ports
      b. St. Lawrence Seaway
      c. Connecting rivers and canals
      d. Boundary with Canada
   5. Mississippi River and its tributaries
      a. Large tributary rivers
      b. Major river ports
      c. New Orleans' rôle

D. Topography and its social influences
   1. Mountain ranges
      a. Appalachians
      b. Rocky Mountains
      c. Ozarks
      d. Sierra Nevadas
      e. Coastal Ranges
      f. Cascade Range
   2. Flat lands
      a. Atlantic Coastal Plain
      b. Gulf Coastal Plain
      c. Central Lowlands
      d. Great Plains
   3. High country
      a. Ozark Plateau
      b. Colorado Plateau
      c. Wyoming Basin
      d. Columbia Plateau
      e. Superior Upland

E. Resources and their locations
   1. Soils
      a. Podzol soils
      b. Gray-brown forest soils

      c. Subtropical red and yellow soils
      d. Prairie soils
      e. Chernozem soils
      f. Desert soils
      g. Mountain and valley soils
   2. Natural vegetation
      a. Coniferous forests
      b. Hardwood forests
      c. Grasslands
   3. Wildlife
      a. Fish
      b. Animals and birds
   4. Minerals
      a. Coal
      b. Iron
      c. Petroleum and natural gas
      d. Other metals and minerals

F. Climates and weather
   1. Zones
      a. Frost
      b. Precipitation
   2. Weather patterns and other phenomena
      a. Air movements
      b. Tropical storms
      c. Arctic influences
      d. Earthquakes and volcanoes
      e. Oceanic influences

G. Economic Regions
   1. The Northeastern Heartland
   2. The South
   3. Interior agricultural and mining region
   4. Western extractive and dryland region
   5. The Far West
   6. Alaska
   7. Hawaiian Islands

III. DISCUSSION PROBLEMS
   1) Inasmuch as the elevations of the Appalachian

Mountains are low by comparative standards, why have their historical effects been so important? What are the most significant of these effects?

2) What outstanding experiences, traditions or habits, and techniques brought to North America by Europeans determined to an important degree the uses made by Americans of their natural environment?

3) Why is the population of the United States so heavily concentrated in certain areas?

4) What climatic and topographical conditions in the United States westward from the 100th meridian have resulted in a sparsity of settlement?

5) How has the proximity of Canada to the United States proved to be an influential factor in Canada's growth?

How has the proximity of Mexico to the United States proved to be an influential factor in Mexico's growth?

6) How do inhabitants of the United States adjust their activities to the averages or means of weather and climate? What are the economic results of such adjustments?

7) What general characteristics of life in the United States stem from the power resources contained in coal, petroleum, and water?

8) Insofar as the United States today is said to be confronting a "farm problem," why is it sometimes stated in terms of surpluses of crops? What explanations can be offered for present-day circumstances? Were these different in earlier periods of history?

9) What importance have the mineral resources of the United States for the development of modern social and economic conditions?

10) What general observations can be applied to the relative balance in the United States of forces and factors working for a rational use of the soil and its resources? For soil conservation? For erosion and wasteful exploitation?

11) What natural highways exist within the United States? What function has each performed throughout history?

IV. STUDY EXERCISES (Maps of the United States)
    Identify and locate the following:
        States and their capitals
        Rivers and major bodies of water
        Crop and livestock regions
        Mineral deposits
        Industrial areas
        Climates and rainfall

V. ADDITIONAL READINGS

R. H. Brown, *Historical Geography of the United States.* New York (Harcourt, Brace), 1948.

G. J. Miller, A. E. Parkins, and B. Hudgins, *The Geography of North America.* New York (Wiley), 1954.

A. J. Wright, *United States and Canada: an Economic Geography.* New York (Appleton-Century-Crofts), 1956.

The New American Nation

I. REQUIRED READINGS

   N. M. Blake, *A Short History of American Life,* pp. 1-141.

   W. Miller, *A History of the United States,* pp. 7-171.

II. MAJOR TOPICS: The New American Nation

   A. *The general problem for students*
      1. To understand the essential features of the 17th-18th century British Empire in North America
      2. To explain the coming of independence for the United States of America

   B. Great Britain's colonies in North America
      1. Uniformity of cultural patterns
         a. Constitutions, governments, and laws
         b. Language and literature
      2. Diversity among the colonies
         a. Churches and religious beliefs
         b. Social philosophy and structures
         c. Natural resources and economic practices

   C. Old World origins of North America's colonials
      1. England, Scotland, Wales, and Ireland
      2. France
      3. Germany
      4. Low Countries
      5. Sweden
      6. Spain and Portugal
      7. Africa

   D. North America's native Indians or Red Men
      1. Migrations from Asia

2. Pre-Columbian distribution and social characteristics
   a. South America
   b. Central America and West Indies
   c. North America
3. Contacts with discoverers, conquerors, and settlers

E. African slaves and European servants
   1. The traffic in African slaves
      a. Slavery in Africa
      b. "Triangular trade"
      c. The passage to America
      d. Plantation labor
   2. Indentured servants from Europe

F. Rivalry for empire in North America
   1. The New World
      a. New England and Nova Scotia
      b. New France
      c. New Netherlands
      d. New Sweden
      e. New Spain
      f. Russian America
   2. Europe's wars and North America's counterparts
      a. Anglo-Dutch Wars
      b. War of the Spanish Succession and Queen Anne's War
      c. War of the Austrian Succession and King George's War
      d. Seven Years' War and the French and Indian War

G. Religious competition in Great Britain's colonies
   1. Major elements
      a. Puritan New England
      b. Roman Catholic Maryland
      c. Quaker Pennsylvania
      d. Church of England
      e. Presbyterianism
      f. Deism and the "Great Awakening"
   2. Effects of religious diversity

H. Colonial arts and the colonial mind
   1. General levels of arts and crafts
   2. Shaping the colonial mind
      a. Puritanism and Christian theology
      b. Enlightenment
      c. Schools and colleges
      d. Anglo-Saxon law
      e. Mercantilism and commerce

I. Independence for the United States of America
   1. The disruption of the British Empire
      a. Divisive questions and constitutional issues
      b. The Declaration of Independence
   2. The War for American Independence
      a. Colonial rebellion
      b. Involvement of France, Spain, and Holland
      c. Independence won
   3. The Constitution of 1787
      a. Reflections of the colonial experience
      b. A federal republic
         1) Separation of powers
         2) Checks and balances
   4. Foreign affairs
      a. Involvements in Anglo-French conflicts to 1815
      b. Purchase of Louisiana territory
      c. War of 1812

III. DISCUSSION PROBLEMS

   1) With what results did commerce, patriotism, and religion conspire to propel the English people into the establishment of colonies in North America?

   2) Is Francis Parkman's description of New France accurate, that "A muskrat, a rosary, and a pack of beaver skins may serve to represent it, and in fact it consisted of little else"?

   3) What techniques of town planning in New England insured that the culture and religion of the original colonies would be carried to new frontiers more or less intact?

   4) What details underlie the observation that Britain's

southern colonies within the area of the future United States afforded a pattern of contrasts?

5) Of what significance was it that influential colonials of the 18th century believed that there is a system of laws belonging to the order of nature to which even sovereigns must bend?

6) Is it possible that an observant traveler could have determined whether he was in New England or Pennsylvania or Virginia by the styles of architecture or furnishings? Of speech or education or religion? Or by any other outward signs of life he encountered?

7) What was important, if anything, about the Great Awakening?

8) What attractions did the Mississippi River have for the *coureurs de bois* besides its grandeur? Is it possible that France once held an advantage over England in the contest for North America?

9) What caused the War of American Independence? What were its immediate and long-term results?

10) What were the fundamental tenets of Jeffersonianism? To what extent did Jefferson's ideas differ from other American patterns of political philosophy and conviction?

11) Why was the United States in trouble with both France and England after 1805? With what results?

IV. STUDY EXERCISES (Declaration of Independence; Constitution)

Study the Declaration of Independence. Analyze this birth certificate of the American nation as: 1) a reflection of the philosophy of the Enlightenment of the 18th century; 2) a statement of the revolutionary case in behalf of independence.

Study the Constitution of 1787. Analyze this fundamental law of the United States: 1) as a product of its historical context; 2) together with the Bill of Rights (Amendments I-X) added in 1791; 3) in an evolutionary setting in the light of all subsequent amendments and developments. Continue your study and analysis of the Constitution as you proceed throughout the entire history of the United States.

V. ADDITIONAL READINGS

J. R. Alden, *The American Revolution.* New York (Harper), 1954.

Vera Brown Holmes, *A History of the Americas.* New York (Ronald), 1950.

C. P. Nettels, *The Roots of American Civilization.* New York (Appleton-Century-Crofts), 1938.

L. B. Wright, *The Cultural Life of the American Colonies,* New York (Harper), 1957.

The Westward Movement

I. REQUIRED READINGS
   N. M. Blake, *A Short History of American Life,* pp. 142-157, 189-317, 336-352.
   W. Miller, *A History of the United States,* pp. 143-205, 265-287.

II. MAJOR TOPICS: The Westward Movement

A. *The general problem for students*
   1. To recognize the main characteristics of the West at the various stages of its development
   2. To understand the significance of the West for the history of the Old World as well as the New

B. Locating the western frontiers
   1. Colonial times (17th-18th centuries)
   2. Early national period (1783-1850)
   3. The last continental frontiers (1850-1912)
   4. The recent past
      a. Alaska and Hawaii
      b. Growth of western populations and influence

C. Westward expansion
   1. Colonial settlements
      a. The Appalachian barrier
      b. New France in the interior
   2. The boundaries of the United States
      a. Treaty limits of 1783
      b. Louisiana Purchase (1803)
      c. Florida Purchase (1819-21)
   3. The Far West
      a. Texas annexation (1845)
      b. Oregon (1846)

13

  c. The War with Mexico (1846-48)
   1) Upper California
   2) New Mexico
  d. Gadsden Purchase (1853)
 4. Alaskan Purchase (1867)
 5. Hawaiian Islands annexation (1898)

D. The westerners
 1. Characteristics of westward migrations throughout America's history
  a. Methods and means of travel
  b. Acquisition of land
  c. Origins of agriculture, commerce, and industry
 2. Effects of migration upon the older regions
  a. Europe
  b. Atlantic seaboard
 3. Origins and folkways of the westerners
  a. Americans from eastern states
   1) New England
   2) Pennsylvania and the Middle Atlantic regions
   3) Virginia, Maryland, and North Carolina
   4) South Carolina and Georgia
  b. Europeans
   1) English and Scotch-Irish
   2) Catholic Irish
   3) Germans
   4) Scandinavians
   5) Others
  c. Asians
   1) Chinese
   2) Japanese
 4. Technology and social institutions
  a. Introduced into the West
  b. Modified by western environmental conditions
 5. Distinguishable stages of western culture
  a. Hunting and foraging
  b. Agriculture, mining, and herding
  c. Industrial and urban complexes
 6. Retarding factors in settling the West
  a. Appalachian Mountains
  b. "Great American Desert"

c. Rocky Mountains and High Sierras
d. Great Plains
1) Indians and wild animals
2) Treeless grasslands

E. The impacts of the West on the older regions of the U.S.A., on Europe, and on Latin America
1. Political
a. Expansion of the U.S.A.
b. From wilderness to statehood
c. Democracy in the West
1) Origins of democracy
2) Rôle of the frontier
2. Economic
a. National resources
b. Products and markets
3. Social and psychological

III. DISCUSSION PROBLEMS

1) To what extent were the upheavals of the era of the French Revolution significant for the United States?

2) Is it either accurate or misleading to regard the history of the frontier as being essentially the history of the westward movement of the population?

3) Is it accurate to say that the political development from wilderness to statehood prescribed in the land ordinances of the 1780s successfully overcame the type of problems that led to the American rebellion against the British Empire?

4) In the developments leading up to the Louisiana Purchase, what explains Jefferson's anxiety over the fate of New Orleans, and his determination to seek an alliance with Great Britain against France if necessary?

5) Why did Andrew Jackson's foray into Florida outrage Great Britain, Spain, and many leading citizens of the United States? Whom did it please?

6) What did the Monroe Doctrine attempt? What did it accomplish?

7) What is to be understood by the remarks of men of sober judgment that the crisis which led to the Missouri Compromise was the most ominous threat that had ever faced the Union?

8) Of what importance for the expansion of the United States was the China trade? "Oregon fever"? The Santa Fe trails? The Mexican War? California gold?

9) What purposes were behind the West's anxiety for transportation routes to be developed to the East when the Mississippi River system lay southward, where New Orleans offered an outlet, where southern markets existed for grain, meat, mules?

10) What indications are there that the spirit of reform pervaded the United States during the middle period of the 19th century?

11) Is it possible to determine why Americans seemed to be among the most religious of peoples, yet were the most afflicted by religious bickerings?

IV. STUDY EXERCISES (Maps of the United States)

Identify and locate the following:

Santa Fe Trail
Oregon Trail
Sacramento
49° N.
36° 30′ N.
Texas
East Florida
West Florida
New Orleans
Cincinnati
St. Louis
Northwest Territory
Missouri
Louisiana Purchase Territory
Utah
Erie Canal
Welland Canal
Soo Canal
Pennsylvania Main Line Canal
Baltimore & Ohio R.R.

V. ADDITIONAL READINGS

R. A. Billington, *Westward Expansion*. New York (Macmillan), 1960.

F. Parkman, *The Oregon Trail,* New York (New American Library), 1950.

R. E. Riegel, *America Moves West.* New York (Holt), 1956.

H. N. Smith, *Virgin Land.* New York (Vintage), 1957.

F. J. Turner, *The Frontier in American History.* New York (Holt), 1920, 1962.

W. P. Webb, *The Great Plains,* New York (Ginn), 1931; and New York (Grosset and Dunlap), 1957.

The Struggle for Southern Independence

II. MAJOR TOPICS: The Struggle for Southern Independence

A. *The general problem for students*
1. To understand the trends leading toward southern secession and potential independence for the South
2. To identify the reasons for the defeat of the Confederacy and the triumph of the Union
3. To recognize the devastating nature of the Civil War and the near-revolutionary effects of the war and its outcome
4. To realize what have been the long-range results for the American people

B. Southern secession and the Civil War
1. The federal union in 1860
a. Powers and policies of the central government
b. Sovereignty of the states
2. The secession movement (eleven states)
a. Lower South
b. Upper South
c. Confederate States of America
d. Repercussions in Missouri, Kentucky, Virginia, Maryland, and elsewhere
3. The outbreak of the Civil War
a. Secession as the precipitating cause
b. War aims of the Federal Government
1) Restoration of the Union
2) Emancipation of the slaves

C. Political aspects of the intersectional crisis
  1. The Constitution
    a. Powers of the central government
    b. Powers reserved to the states
  2. The courts of highest appeal in theory and practice
    a. Nationalism
      1) Popular majority
      2) Supremacy of the Constitution
      3) President, Congress, and Supreme Court
    b. States-rights positions
      1) Kentucky and Virginia Resolves (1798)
      2) South Carolina's nullification doctrine (1832-33)
      3) Senator John C. Calhoun's theory of the "concurrent majority" (1850)
      4) Secessionism (1860-61)

D. Economic divergences between North and South
  1. South
    a. Agrarian and rural
    b. Staple crops for export
    c. Slave labor
  2. North
    a. Industrialization and urbanization
    b. Homestead farms and variegated agriculture
    c. Attractive for immigrants
  3. Transportation and commerce
    a. North-South trade routes
    b. East-West canals and railroads

E. Social philosophies and institutions
  1. Sectional stereotypes
    a. Aristocratic South
    b. Democratic North
    c. Democratic West
  2. Slavery
    a. Possibly the fundamental cause of the trouble between North and South
    b. Characteristics
      1) Plantation labor
      2) Domestic traffic in slaves

3) International trade and prohibition
c. Antislavery agitation
d. South's defense of slavery
e. Fugitive-slave questions

F. The West and the coming of the Civil War
1. Slavery and western disputes
    a. Missouri Compromise (1820)
    b. Texas annexation question (1836-45)
    c. Mexican War (1846-48)
    d. Compromise of 1850
2. Entry of California as a free state
3. "Bleeding" Kansas
4. Election of Abraham Lincoln (1860)

G. The Civil War
1. Conditions of victory and defeat
    a. North
        1) Persistence to destroy rebellion
        2) Superior resources
    b. South
        1) Defense of areas in rebellion
        2) Foreign recognition and aid
        3) Northern weariness and distaste for costs of war
2. Military trends toward Union victory
    a. Blockade of Confederacy and capture of ports
    b. Splitting the South and conquering the separate portions
    c. Destroying southern industry and manpower
3. Meaning of the Union's victory
    a. North
        1) Triumph of American democratic nationalism
        2) Victory for industrial and urban forces
    b. South—defeat of separatism
4. "Reconstruction" of the South
    a. Military occupation and humiliation
    b. Ex-slaves
    c. Heritage in South of bitter hatreds

III. DISCUSSION PROBLEMS

1) Analyze the features of Southern society that distinguished it from the North.

2) What arguments were employed to defend the institution of slavery against the attacks of antislavery forces?

3) Is it true that innovations in manufacturing, transportation, and commerce brought on the Civil War?

4) Why and on what issues during the 1850s did the spirit of compromise fail to achieve workable results?

5) What considerations in 1861 as the Civil War commenced might have prompted a Southern anticipation of victory?

6) Why was a long war likely to prove advantageous to the North?

7) What were the costs and consequences of the Civil War for the United States?

8) Why can it be affirmed that the heaviest blow to the stricken South was the moral cost of war and defeat and ultimately of Reconstruction?

9) In what sense was the American Civil War unusual among wars of the 19th century?

10) How might modern realization of the problems of under-developed and war-ravaged countries help us to understand the South's prostration after the Civil War?

11) Of what importance were the 13th, 14th, and 15th Amendments to the Constitution?

12) What developments became characteristic of the post-Civil War South?

IV. STUDY EXERCISES (Maps of the United States)

Identify and locate the following:

Missouri Compromise

California

Gadsden purchase

Territory acquired from Mexico (1848)

Kansas Territory

Harper's Ferry

Fort Sumter

Cotton Kingdom

Tobacco country
Sugar region
Confederate States of America
Washington, D.C.
Richmond
Charleston
Atlanta
Savannah
Antietam
Gettysburg
Nashville
Chattanooga
Vicksburg
St. Louis
Cincinnati
Union slave states
New Orleans
Ohio River
Mississippi River

V. ADDITIONAL READINGS

S. V. Benet, *John Brown's Body*, New York (Rinehart), 1954.

W. J. Cash, *The Mind of the South*, New York (Knopf), 1941, (Vintage), 1960.

L. Filler, *The Crusade against Slavery*, New York (Harper), 1960.

J. G. Randall, *The Civil War and Reconstruction*, rev. ed. by David Donald, Boston (Heath), 1961.

F. B. Simkins, *A History of the South*, New York (Knopf), 1953.

R. P. Warren, *The Legacy of the Civil War*, New York (Random House), 1961.

C. V. Woodward, *Origins of the New South*, Baton Rouge (Louisiana State University), 1951.

The Dynamics of Social Change

I. REQUIRED READINGS
   N. M. Blake, *A Short History of American Life*, pp. 375-552.
   W. Miller, *A History of the United States*, pp. 288-353.

II. MAJOR TOPICS: The Dynamics of Social Change

A. *The general problem for students*
   1. To identify the major forces for stability, change, and growth which shaped the early history of the U.S.A.
   2. To note those developments which would become characteristic of American society in the 20th century
   3. To recognize the blend of resources and social dynamics which brought industrialism to the U.S.A.
   4. To understand the domestic social and economic revolution wrought by the industrialization of the U.S.A., together with its worldwide effects

B. The perspectives of American history

C. Industry's revolution begins in the Northern states
   1. Natural resources, labor, and capital
   2. Textiles
   3. Iron and steel
   4. Agricultural machinery
   5. Roads, canals, steamboats
   6. Railroads—the most dynamic factor
      a. Construction and operation
      b. Eastern network by 1860
      c. Transcontinental railroads
D. Railroads and the industrial revolution

23

　　1. Governmental policies
　　　　a. Public lands
　　　　b. Financial assistance
　　　　c. Absence of regulation
　　2. Corporate form of organization
　　　　a. Private businessmen and their partners
　　　　b. Corporation stocks and bonds
　　　　c. Finance
　　3. Relationships to developments in other industries
　　　　a. Mining and lumbering
　　　　b. Extraction of metals and minerals
　　　　c. Iron and steel
　　　　d. Communications
　　　　e. Agriculture and animal husbandry
　　　　f. Meat packing and dairying
　　　　g. Electrical industry
　　　　h. Petroleum extraction and refining

E. Social philosophy and the corporation
　　1. Rapid and spectacular developments
　　　　a. Rise of the "captains" of industry and finance
　　　　b. Size and complexity of corporations
　　　　c. Trend toward combinations and monopoly
　　2. Public attitudes
　　　　a. Private property and the law
　　　　b. Individualism and democracy
　　　　c. Heritage of puritanism
　　　　d. Belief in progress and *laissez-faire* policies
　　3. Emergence of regulatory philosophies and policies
　　　　a. Delayed by
　　　　　　1) Federal organization of U.S.A.
　　　　　　2) Ambivalence of public attitudes
　　　　b. Beginnings
　　　　　　1) Protests and reform movements
　　　　　　2) Agrarian distress
　　　　　　3) Interstate commerce

F. Immigration
　　1. Sources of colonial population
　　2. Novel ingredients

      a. Roman Catholic Irish
      b. Germans in increasing numbers
      c. Scandinavians
      d. Massive waves of European immigrants (1880-1914)
   3. Significant aspects
      a. Scope and composition of immigration
      b. Motives of immigrants in choosing to come to the U.S.A.
      c. Effects of migrations
         1) Upon homelands
         2) Upon U.S.A., especially as an additional dynamic factor during the industrial revolution
      d. Developments in official policy toward immigration
      e. Present policy and conditions

G. Urbanization—the rise of city life
   1. Cities of the U.S.A.
      a. Older commercial cities
      b. New industrial cities
   2. Patterns and problems of city life
      a. Rapidity of growth
      b. Immigrants and farmers
      c. Local government

III. DISCUSSION PROBLEMS

    1) Who were the immigrants of the 1840s and 1850s, and why did they come to the United States? Of the 1870s? Of the early 20th century?

    2) Which national or ethnic groups of immigrants settled at once in cities, and why? Which groups chose farming?

    3) Explain the importance of Chicago, New York City, and Pittsburgh.

    4) What indications are there of the immaturity of American industry before 1850?

    5) Of what importance for American society was the warm welcome given to the philosophy of Herbert Spencer?

6) Was there some peculiarity of Southern society that resisted the coming of industrialism?

7) Describe and explain the relationships which developed between the railroads and government.

8) What was the Wild West? Why has it entered so indelibly into the American spirit and mythology?

9) Explain the purposes and techniques of: a) a pool; b) a trust; c) a holding company; d) a corporation.

10) Evaluate the importance of innovations in the communications and electrical industries around 1900.

11) What were the distinctive features of the American labor movement? Of the Railway Brotherhoods? Of the Knights of Labor? Of the American Federation of Labor? Of the American Railway Union? Of the Industrial Workers of the World?

12) How did the arrival of new immigrants aggravate the difficulties of city life with which Americans were already struggling?

13) What developments entangled the American farmer in the world's commerce? How did he react?

IV. STUDY EXERCISES (Maps of the United States and Europe) Identify and locate the following:

Places of European immigrant origin
Places of immigrant destination

Great Plains
Major farm crop areas
Areas of Populist strength

Transcontinental railroads
Major cities (ca. 1900)
Iron and steel industry
Coal production centers
Oil production centers
Electrical industry
Automotive industry

V. ADDITIONAL READINGS

T. C. Cochran and W. Miller, *The Age of Enterprise,* New York (Macmillan), 1942, (Harper), 1961.

M. A. Jones, *American Immigration*, Chicago (University of Chicago), 1960.

E. C. Kirkland, *Industry Comes of Age*, New York (Holt, Rinehart, and Winston), 1961.

F. A. Shannon, *The Farmer's Last Frontier*, New York (Farrar and Rinehart), 1945.

The Rise to World Power

I. REQUIRED READING
I. REQUIRED READING

N. M. Blake, *A Short History of American Life,* pp. 553-688.

W. Miller, *A History of the United States,* pp. 354-484.

II. MAJOR TOPICS: The Rise to World Power

A. *The general problem for students*
   1. To understand the historic currents of life in the U.S.A. during the recent past
   2. To recognize the parts played by the U.S.A. and its citizens in world developments during the 20th century
   3. To assess the results for the American people of the global social changes transforming human affairs

B. Global upheavals of the 20th century
   1. Wars, famines, and epidemics
   2. Economic turbulence
      a. Spectacular growth of production and populations
      b. Depressions and destitution
      c. Spread of industrialism
   3. Social revolutions
   4. Scientific and technological breakthroughs

C. American foreign policy and outlooks in the 19th century
   1. Continental expansionism and "manifest destiny"
   2. Monroe Doctrine and isolationism
      a. Doctrine of the two hemispheres (1823)
         1) Latin American independence movements
         2) Great Britain and the Holy Alliance

b. Great Britain and France during the Civil War
c. Growing interests in Latin America, China, and Japan
3. War against Spain (1898) and its aftermath
a. The U.S.A. as a world power
1) Defeat of Spain
2) Annexation of Hawaiian Islands
3) Control over Cuba, Puerto Rico, and Philippine Islands
b. Panama Canal
c. "Open Door" policy for China
d. "Dollar Diplomacy"
e. Rise of Imperial Japan

D. The U.S.A. and the First World War (1914-1918)
1. Tensions of American neutrality
2. Entry on the side of Great Britain and France (1917)
a. Reasons for war against Germany
b. Effects of U.S. participation
3. Rejection of the League of Nations

E. The U.S.A. between the great wars
1. Deepening mood of isolationism
a. Barriers to immigration
b. Aloofness from international organizations
c. Problems of war debts and reparations
d. Fear of Communism
2. Technological and social transformations
a. Mass production and mass consumption
b. Wider democracy
c. Relativism and the impact of Freudianism
3. Great depression of 1930s
a. Collapse of U.S. economy
b. Worldwide economic catastrophe
c. New Deal

F. The U.S.A. and the Second World War (1939-1945)
1. Threats from totalitarianisms: Germany, Japan, Italy, Russia

2. Fall of France brought U.S.A. to war's edge
3. Japan's attack on Pearl Harbor (1941)
4. The road to victory
   a. Roosevelt and Churchill
   b. Uneasy partnership with Russia
   c. Miracles of production
   d. Defeats in turn of Italy, Germany, Japan
   e. Dawn of atomic warfare
5. United Nations (1945)

G. The Cold War
   1. Collapse of the Grand Alliance
      a. "Iron curtain"
      b. Russia against the West
   2. U.S. policy of "containment" of Communism
      a. Truman Doctrine and Marshall Plan
      b. North Atlantic Treaty Organization (1949)
      c. Mutual security and aid programs
      d. Problem of Germany
   3. Turbulence in the Orient
      a. Chinese revolution (1949)
      b. Korean War (1950)
      c. Indochina
         1) Laos
         2) Viet-Nam
         3) Cambodia
      d. Indonesia, Malaya, Burma, India, Pakistan
      e. Nationalisms and Communism
   4. Africa
      a. New nations emerging
      b. Algerian independence
      c. Egypt and the United Arab Republic
   5. Middle East
      a. Oil
      b. Arab and Jew
   6. Latin America
   7. Contemporary developments
      a. Characteristics of U.S. foreign policy
      b. Dangers of thermonuclear warfare
      c. Penetration of outer space

H. Recent economic developments
  1. The prosperity of the 1920s
      a. Industrial boom
          1) Automobiles and household appliances
          2) Electrochemical enterprises
      b. Weak spots in agriculture and some industries
      c. Wall Street crash of 1929 and Great Depression of 1930s
  2. The New Deal and economic recovery
      a. Banking, money, and securities
      b. Relief—aid to the unemployed
      c. Planning for industry and agriculture
      d. Welfare-state reforms
      e. Governmental assumption of responsibility for prosperity
  3. The Second World War
      a. "Arsenal of democracy"
      b. Technological advances
  4. The post-war economic breakthrough
      a. Worldwide upheavals
          1) New nations
          2) Population explosion and mass poverty
          3) Competition between U.S.A. and U.S.S.R.
      b. Industrial revolution continuing in U.S.A.
          1) Vast increase in scale and variety of production
          2) Research and development
          3) Chemicals and electronics industries
          4) Automation
      c. The challenges of unlimited economic growth
          1) Management
          2) Social responsibility

III. DISCUSSION PROBLEMS
    1) Why did certain European powers enter a new imperialist phase around 1900? To what degree did Japan participate? To what degree did the United States participate?
    2) How and why was the United States involved in Far Eastern power relationships by 1912?

3) What was the diplomatic and political background for the construction of the Panama Canal? Of what importance have the canal and related matters been ever since?

4) Why did the United States choose to fight Germany in 1917?

5) Did the League of Nations reflect either the war aims or the popular ideals of the American people? Why did the United States fail to join?

6) What were the major provisions and results of America's immigration policy as adopted during the 1920s?

7) What were the outstanding features of governmental philosophy and policy during the Great Depression of the 1930s?

8) Why and with what results did artists and writers of the "lost generation" feel alienated from society? The "beat generation"?

9) What was the importance for the United States of the defeat of France in May-June 1940?

10) What was the Allies' grand strategy of World War II? Was it a satisfactory conception of the conditions and problems at hand?

11) What have been the most impressive achievements of recent science and technology? What problems have these developments solved or created?

12) What were the results of World War II for the world and the United States?

13) What issues or forces caused the Cold War? What have been its results so far?

14) What exactly did the New Deal government of President Roosevelt do that created so much domestic controversy? What have been its lingering effects?

15) What, to employ Joseph Schumpeter's terminology, had capitalism's "perennial gale of creative destruction" to do with post-war economic changes in America? What was the significance of governmental activity?

IV. STUDY EXERCISES (Maps of the World)
  Identify and locate the following:
    Pearl Harbor

Aleutian Islands
Samoa
Manila Bay
Panama Canal
Vera Cruz, Mexico
Portsmouth, N.H.
San Francisco
Area of the Open Door policy
Areas of Dollar Diplomacy
Area of the Platt Amendment
Area of the Monroe Doctrine
Organization of American States
38th Parallel
Geneva
Midway Island
N.A.T.O.
S.E.A.T.O.
C.E.N.T.O.
Formosa
New York City

V. ADDITIONAL READINGS

T. A. Bailey, *A Diplomatic History of the American People*, New York (Appleton-Century-Crofts), 1958.

N. M. Blake and O. T. Barck, *The United States in Its World Relations*, New York (McGraw-Hill), 1960.

J. Davids, *America and the World of Our Time*, New York (Random House), 1960.

F. R. Dulles, *America's Rise to World Power*, New York (Harper), 1954.

H. W. Gatzke, *The Present in Perspective*, New York (Rand McNally), 1961.

G. F. Kennan, *American Diplomacy, 1900-1950*, Chicago (University of Chicago), 1951.

E. C. Rozwenc, *The New Deal: Revolution or Evolution?* rev. ed., Boston (Heath), 1959.

Part A: Review

A. *The general problem for students* is to think over thoroughly and systematically what forces and factors of geography and history have combined to produce the present characteristics of life in the U.S.A.

B. Natural conditions
   1. Topography and contours
   2. Climates
      a. Precipitation and frost zones
      b. Weather patterns and variations
   3. Resources
      a. Soils and water
      b. Vegetation
      c. Minerals
      d. Wildlife

C. Immigration and settlement
   1. Native American Indians
   2. Immigration by stages
      a. Colonial population
      b. Africans
      c. Northwestern Europeans
      d. Eastern and southern Europeans
      e. Oriental peoples
   3. Importation of Old World social practices, institutions, and beliefs
      a. Family and societal relationships
      b. Concepts of property and law
      c. Religious beliefs and churches
      d. Languages, literature, and systems of philosophy
      e. Agricultural and business practices

35

      f. Science and technology
      g. Fine arts
      h. Education
    4. Public policies on immigration

D. Anglo-American hegemony and its importance
    1. Land
      a. Distribution and ownership
      b. Exploitation and cultivation
    2. Law, politics, and government
    3. Social structures
      a. Religion
      b. Business
      c. Education
      d. Family life
    4. Modifications by diverse immigrant groups, ideas, and institutions

E. Federalism
    1. Government
      a. The U.S.A. as a Federal Union
      b. Federal-state relationships and conflicts
      c. Dispersion of rights, powers, responsibilities
      d. The Constitution
    2. Localism
      a. Education
      b. Religion
      c. Business
      d. Police powers and regulations
    3. Citizenship

F. Commerce and industry
    1. Natural resources
    2. Capitalism and enterprise
    3. Governmental policy
      a. Federal, state, and local
      b. Assistance and support
      c. Regulation and control
    4. Rise of the corporation
    5. Agriculture

      a. Plantations
      b. Homestead farms
      c. Commercialization and mechanization
      d. "Scientific" farming today
   6. Labor
      a. Colonial patterns: free, indentured, slave
      b. Individualistic and opportunistic
      c. Relatively scarce and costly
      d. Growth of unions and their characteristics
   7. Business practices and circumstances
      a. Philosophy of business
      b. Size, scope, and range of services
   8. Leading industries
      a. Textiles
      b. Building construction
      c. Iron and steel
      d. Railroads
      e. Electrical
      f. Chemical
      g. Automobiles and appliances
      h. Aluminum and light metals

G. Foreign policies and determinations
   1. Historical periods
      a. From 1776 to 1823
      b. From 1823 to 1898
      c. From 1898 to 1920
      d. From 1920 to 1939
      e. Since 1939. . . . .
   2. Conditions and outlooks
      a. Geographic factors
      b. World power politics
      c. Philosophic viewpoints
      d. Ethnic components of U.S. population

H. Democracy
   1. Historical growth or spread of democracy
      a. Aids to acceptance of democratic ideals and practices
      b. Retarding factors

    1) Sex
    2) Race
    3) Tradition
  2. Triumph of democracy
   a. Politics
   b. Economic activity
   c. Religion and education
   d. Social customs and attitudes
  3. The liberties and rights of the people of the U.S.A.
   a. Evolution to present conditions
   b. The Constitution, the Bill of Rights, and the judicial process

 I. Summary: geography and history
  1. The land and its people
  2. The American nation

II. THE GROWTH OF THE AMERICAN NATION
  By means of a map show the territorial growth of the U.S.A., and identify the fifty states of the Federal Union.

Part B: Living Ideas and Institutions

The Federal System

I. REQUIRED READINGS
H. Zink, H. R. Penniman, and G. B. Hathorn, *American Government and Politics*, pp. 1-74, 136-226, 328-430.

II. MAJOR TOPICS: The Federal System

A. *The general problem for students* is to understand the practical everyday workings of the principles of government in the U.S.A.
1. Republicanism
2. Democracy
3. Federalism and the separation of powers
   a. The Federal system of state and national government
   b. Checks and balances
4. Constitutionalism

B. Federalism in principle and practice: dual nature of government
1. Federal government
   a. Capital at Washington, D.C.
   b. National powers
   c. National agencies
2. Fifty state governments
   a. Local powers
   b. Organized like the Federal government

C. The separation of powers
1. The Federal system
   a. National government
   b. State governments
2. Checks and balances
   a. Executive powers

41

      b. Legislative powers and bicameralism
      c. Judicial powers
    3. Compromises and conflicts
      a. Local government and central authority
      b. Executives and legislators
      c. Judges as supreme lawgivers

D. The Constitution of the United States of America
    1. The Constitution of 1787
      a. Preamble
      b. Article I: legislative powers
      c. Article II: executive power
      d. Article III: judicial power
      e. Article IV: full faith and credit
      f. Article V: process of amendment
      g. Article VI: miscellany
         1) Validation of prior debts and contracts
         2) Supreme law of the land
         3) Public officials' oath or affirmation to support this Constitution
      h. Article VII: ratification
    2. Amendments to the Constitution
      a. Amendments I-X (Bill of Rights, 1791)
      b. Amendments XI-XXIII (1798-1961)
    3. The unwritten Constitution: amendment by interpretation and evolving practice
    4. Powers of the Federal government
      a. Enumerated powers
      b. Implied powers

E. Dual citizenship
    1. Amendment XIV of the Constitution
    2. Means by which persons become
      a. Citizens of the U.S.A.
      b. Citizens of states
    3. Rights and duties of citizenship
    4. Foreign-born persons
      a. Resident aliens
      b. Naturalization
      c. Rights and duties of foreign-born persons

F. The Federal laws and powers
   1. Congress legislates matters into law
      a. House of Representatives
      b. Senate
      c. Taxation and appropriations
   2. President executes laws
      a. Signs Congressional actions into law
      b. Guides public policy, administers public acts, and conducts foreign relations
      c. Powers of appointment
      d. Commander-in-chief of the armed forces
   3. Courts
      a. Enforce laws
      b. Appeals procedures
   4. Veto powers
      a. Congress
         1) Approval of both branches required for passage of pending bills
         2) Two-thirds vote required to override a presidential veto
      b. President
         1) Rejection of Congressional bills
         2) "Pocket veto"
      c. Supreme Court and "judicial review"

G. The laws and powers of the states
   1. "Sovereignty" of each of the states
      a. The federal system
      b. Article IV of the Constitution: full faith and credit
      c. Powers reserved to the states (Amendment X)
   2. Relationships between the states and the Federal government
   3. Governmental process in the states similar to that of the Federal government
   4. Subdivisions of state governments
      a. Counties
      b. Townships, villages, and cities
      c. School districts
   5. Supremacy of states in "domestic" matters

    a. Marriage and divorce
    b. Real and personal property
    c. Police regulations
    d. Community services

III. DISCUSSION PROBLEMS

1) Explain the relationships to each other, legal or otherwise, of the Continental Congress, the Annapolis Convention, and the Philadelphia Convention of 1787.

2) If, as is true, the power of judicial review is nowhere mentioned in the Constitution, how has it developed? Is it legal?

3) What characteristics of the Constitution have permitted it to adapt to national growth and change?

4) What philosophy of government and its powers was embodied in the Federal Bill of Rights? Of what importance today are the particular matters dealt with by the first ten amendments?

5) What is to be understood by the observation that the United States has "presidential government"?

6) If the separate states are indeed "sovereign," how can the Constitution, laws, and treaties of the United States be "the supreme law of the land"?

7) Explain the process by which new states have been admitted to the Union, and the relationships arising between new states and old. What is the significance of this process?

8) What are the obligations of the states to sister states? What sort of problems arise in the area of interstate relations?

9) What has been the importance of immigration to the United States? How did immigration itself tend to produce the prevailing laws on citizenship, naturalization, and entry quotas?

10) What is the difference between procedural and substantive due process of law?

11) How has the Cabinet developed to present circumstances without either Constitutional or general statutory authority?

12) What are the leading general characteristics of

state government in the United States? Of local government?

13) Generally speaking, what types of problems are of greatest importance for America's municipalities? Of what help or hindrance are the state governments? The Federal government?

IV. STUDY EXERCISES

Prepare diagrams to illustrate the following:

Separation of powers
Checks and balances
Judicial review
Conduct of foreign relations
Federal-state relationships

V. ADDITIONAL READINGS

C. A. Beard, *An Economic Interpretation of the Constitution*, New York (Macmillan), 1935.

E. S. Corwin, ed., *The Constitution of the United States of America*, Washington (Government Printing Office), 1953.

R. Hofstadter, *The American Political Tradition*, New York (Knopf), 1948.

A. H. Kelly and W. A. Harbison, *The American Constitution*, New York (Norton), 1955.

J. C. Miller, *The Federalist Era*, New York (Harper), 1960.

C. L. Rossiter, *The American Presidency*, New York (Harcourt, Brace), 1960.

Government and Politics

II. MAJOR TOPICS: Government and Politics

A. *The general problem for students*
   1. To recognize the basic features of the political process in the U.S.A., and to know how these have evolved to present-day conditions
   2. To determine the practical working connections on all levels between politics and government
   3. To identify the relationships between
      a. Voters and political parties
      b. Officeholders and political parties
      c. Majority and minority parties
   4. To seek an understanding of what determines whether Americans will be either Republicans or Democrats

B. Politics in the U.S.A.
   1. The total political process at work
      a. Politics
      b. Government
   2. Evolutionary developments
      a. Increasing democracy
         1) Voting
         2) Officeholding
      b. History of political parties
         1) Major national parties
         2) Minor parties
         3) Parties and the Constitution

    c. Growing size, strength, and importance of government

C. Voting and elective officeholding
  1. Successive impacts of growing democracy
    a. Requirements and opportunities for voting and officeholding
      1) Property
      2) Race or creed
    b. Importance of public opinion
  2. Voting and officeholding
    a. Requisites for voting
    b. Requisites for officeholding
      1) In general
      2) For candidates for U.S. Representative and U.S. Senator
      3) For President and Vice-President
    c. Patterns and motives of non-voting
  3. Voting procedures
    a. Conduct of elections
    b. Timing of elections
      1) Every four years
      2) Every two years
      3) At other intervals
    c. Legal requirements

D. Public opinion
  1. Radio, television, and motion pictures
  2. Newspapers and public opinion polls
  3. Lobbyists and pressure groups
  4. Petitions, telegrams, letters, processions, and picketing
  5. Sensitivity of elected officials

E. Political parties
  1. Extra-Constitutional development
    a. Historical background
    b. Assumption of nominating and electioneering process
  2. Democratic party
    a. Origins and evolution
    b. Present characteristics

      c. Northern Democrats and Southern Democrats

   3. Republican party

      a. Origins and evolution

      b. Present characteristics

      c. Conservative and liberal Republicans

   4. Functions and purposes of two major parties

      a. Compromises among factions

         1) Regional and class interests

         2) Attitudes on domestic and foreign policies

         3) National and local issues

      b. Implementation of the Constitution and the Federal system

         1) Selection of candidates

         2) Presentation of issues

         3) Appeals to voters

         4) Responsible leadership and opposition in government

      c. Distinctions between local and national functions

   5. Minor or third parties

      a. Historical record

      b. Present characteristics

      c. Tendencies toward

         1) Loss of appeal because major parties take their popular issues

         2) Disappearance

F. Administration and bureaucracy

   1. Federal, state, and local levels

   2. The Federal Government

      a. The Cabinet

         1) Historical evolution

         2) Powers and duties

         3) Relationships to the President

      b. Hierarchy of organizations

         1) Departments

         2) Bureaus and agencies, etc.

      c. Executive Office of the President

         1) Advisers and assistants
           Budget and finances

         2) Administration

         3) Planning policy and strategy

    d. The President
        1) Chief Executive
        2) Commander-in-chief and foreign relations
        3) Head of his political party
        4) Relations with Congress
        5) Power of appointments

G. Taxation
    1. General view of taxation
        a. Absolute and comparative levels of tax burdens between U.S.A. and other countries
        b. Allocations in U.S.A. of specific tax revenues
    2. National taxes
        a. Income tax
        b. Tariffs on imports
        c. Excise taxes
    3. State and local taxes
        a. Excise taxes
        b. Sales and purchase taxes
        c. Real estate and property taxes
        d. Roads, sewers, and schools taxes

III. DISCUSSION PROBLEMS

1) How has the system of political parties helped the Constitution to work out in practice?

2) What reasoning and developments have produced the long and complicated procedures for choosing a President of the United States?

3) What useful points of comparison and contrast with practices in other countries can serve to illustrate the peculiar features of the office of President of the United States?

4) Why do the major political parties of the United States sometimes appear to be almost indistinguishable from one another? Are they?

5) How democratic is the political process in the United States? What does the Federal government do to ensure voting? What is the function of the states at election times?

6) What political and voting reforms have been ac-

complished over the years? What conditions produced them?

7) How is public opinion created in the United States? How is it assessed? How does it become effective?

8) How would you rank the major administrative departments of the Federal government in order of importance? What criteria determine the order of your listing?

9) Does patronage or the "spoils system" play any part in the functioning of government in the United States?

10) By comparison with other peoples, how heavily are Americans taxed? To what extent does the pattern of Federal and State taxation complicate understanding of this point?

11) Does the Federal Reserve System perform the functions of a central bank? What is the purpose of the Treasury Department?

IV. STUDY EXERCISES

Prepare diagrams to illustrate the following:

Executive branch of the Federal government including Cabinet departments, regulatory commissions, and major agencies.

Legislative branch of the Federal government including the functions and major committees of both houses of Congress.

Judicial branch of the Federal government including the various levels of courts and their jurisdictions.

V. ADDITIONAL READINGS

W. E. Binkley, *American Political Parties*, New York (Knopf), 1958.

D. W. Brogan, *Politics in America*, New York (Harper), 1954.

E. S. Corwin, *The President: Office and Powers*, New York (New York University), 1957.

R. Hofstadter, *The Age of Reform*, New York (Knopf), 1955.

A. M. Schlesinger Jr., *The Age of Jackson*, Boston (Little, Brown), 1945.

The Business Outlook

II. MAJOR TOPICS: The Business Outlook

A. *The general problem for students*
1. To determine the characteristics of business in the U.S.A.
2. To define the place occupied by businessmen in American society
3. To show the relative power and prominence of business in American life compared to other countries and regions
   a. Great Britain and the British Commonwealth
   b. Western Europe
   c. Latin America
   d. Africa
   e. Japan
   f. Russia, Communist China and other Communist states

B. Business and businessmen
1. The U.S.A. as a "business society"
   a. Influence of businessmen upon government and social institutions
   b. Prestige of business and businessmen
   c. Business and the economy as a whole
2. Business and technological development
   a. Factors influencing technological advancement or retardation
   b. Problems of capital accumulation
   c. Business and labor

51

C. Characteristics of business in the U.S.A.
  1. Small businesses
     a. Specialty manufacturing, sales, and services
     b. Construction
     c. Individual ownership or partnership
     d. Local markets
  2. Medium to large businesses
     a. Manufacturing, wholesale selling, retailing
     b. Banking and insurance
     c. Transportation
     d. Construction
     e. Corporate form of organization
     f. Local, regional, or national markets depending on size and nature of enterprise
  3. Giant corporations
     a. Manufacturing
     b. Banking and insurance
     c. Transportation
     d. Tens of thousands of employees and shareholders; professional managers
     e. Enormous fiscal resources, income, and expenditures
     f. National to worldwide markets
     g. Major suppliers for governmental purchases
     h. Share of the nation's business
  4. The "voice" of business
     a. Small businessmen
        1) Most numerous
        2) Articulate, active, and influential
     b. Giant corporations and public relations
     c. Relationships and attitudes regarding business and government a significant factor

D. Business and technological development
  1. General consideration of technology's impacts on American business and society
  2. Major industrial developments
     a. Textiles manufacturing
     b. Iron and steel
     c. Railroads
     d. Electrical industry

e. Chemicals manufacturing
f. Automobiles and household appliances
g. Electronics industry
h. Defense industries
3. Important factors
   a. Natural resources
   b. Imitation and borrowing from Europe
   c. Invention and promotion
   d. Mass production and mass consumption
      1) Interchangeable parts
      2) Continuous-flow assembly line
      3) Automation
      4) Enlargement of markets
4. Technology and society: some topics and problems
   a. Employment and displacement of labor
   b. Rising material standards of living
   c. Labor-saving devices and emphasis
   d. Machines and human values
   e. Business cycles and technological innovation

E. Rise of the corporations
  1. Significant epochs in economic history
    a. Feudalism of Middle Ages
    b. Commerce and mercantilism
    c. Industrial revolution
    d. Corporations
  2. Trend toward corporations
    a. Early 19th century
    b. Reasons
       1) Raising large resources of capital
       2) Sharing the risks
       3) Conducting far-flung and intricate operations
  3. Modern business corporations
    a. Ownership separated from control
       1) Shareholders
       2) Professional managers
       3) The corporate identity and image
    b. Taxation
       1) Income tax on corporate profits
       2) Shareholders' dividends and earnings subject
         to tax on individual incomes

　　　　3) Employees' wages taxed individually
　　c. Dominating non-governmental element in U.S. economy
　　d. Various degrees of governmental regulation
　　　　1) Chartered and regulated by states
　　　　2) Interstate commerce subject to Federal regulations
　　　　3) Antitrust laws
　　e. Scientific management

F. Business and the values of American society
　1. Religious and democratic traditions
　2. Business and group interests
　　a. Farmers
　　b. Wage earners
　　c. Other groups
　3. Business and national opinion
　　a. Sympathy and support
　　b. Antagonism and conflicts

III. DISCUSSION PROBLEMS

1) Why is it, when compared with the businessmen of other nations, that those of the United States have always enjoyed great social prestige?

2) Of what importance has it been for ideas and attitudes concerning business that, in the big corporations today, ownership is separated from control?

3) What theoretical as well as practical difficulties confront the managers of big business seeking to justify their great powers to the public?

4) Why did the American economy swing so violently from prosperity to deep depression and back again as it did in the years 1929 to 1955?

5) What are the laws in the United States against "monopoly," "trusts," and "restraint of trade"? How effective have they been? What is public opinion on this subject?

6) How did it happen that, at the beginning of the 20th century after an era of massive achievement, "business" came under attack from the general public and its political representatives?

7) How can the paradox of American business be explained, that of being both highly standardized and infinitely differentiated?

8) What have advertising and public relations to do with business in the United States?

9) To what extent and for what reasons did corporate capitalism in the United States fall under the control of bankers and financiers? With what outcome?

10) Why does it seem today that American business has as little to fear from adverse action by either government or the public as at any previous time in the 20th century?

11) To what extent has there been a failure to reconcile business attitudes and aims, such as the pursuit of an ever higher standard of living, with the other fundamental values stemming from American artistic, religious, and democratic traditions?

12) What factual basis exists for regarding the American business system in the second half of the 20th century as the center of "the big change" or a "permanent revolution"?

13) What were the attitudes of business and businessmen toward President Franklin D. Roosevelt and the New Deal? Can these be explained?

IV. STUDY EXERCISES

Prepare a list to demonstrate comparisons of basic ideas and attitudes between America's businessmen and other social groups.

Prepare a chart along lines of chronological development to illustrate the major characteristics of business in the U.S.A. during the past century or so, including leading industries and the influence of bankers, wars, booms and depressions, technological changes, and governmental policies.

V. ADDITIONAL READINGS

A. A. Berle, Jr., *The 20th Century Capitalist Revolution,* New York (Harcourt, Brace), 1954, 1960.

T. C. Cochran, *Basic History of American Business,* Princeton (Van Nostrand Anvil), 1959.

T. C. Cochran and W. Miller, *The Age of Enterprise,* New York (Macmillan), 1942, (Harper), 1961.

J. F. Dewhurst, *et al., America's Needs and Resources,* New York (20th Century Fund), 1955.

J. K. Galbraith, *The Affluent Society,* Boston (Houghton, Mifflin), 1958.

Religion and the Churches

II. MAJOR TOPICS: Religion and the Churches

A. *The general problem for students*
   1. To recognize the characteristics of religious life in the U.S.A.
   2. To understand how these have evolved to present circumstances

B. The development of religions and churches
   1. Diverse origins of colonial population
   2. Present-day conditions
      a. 19th and 20th century immigration
      b. Ethnic composition of the population
   3. The churches
      a. Dogmas and doctrines
      b. Sectarianism and denominationalism
      c. Patterns of government and authority
      d. Supported by voluntary donations
   4. Government, the churches, and religious beliefs
      a. No established church
      b. First Amendment of the Constitution
   5. U.S.A. basically a Christian nation in religious outlooks and affiliations

C. Historical development of a religiously diversified population
  1. Colonial ingredients
    a. Protestant Christians from Great Britain
      1) Puritans
      2) Presbyterians
      3) Anglicans
      4) Quakers
    b. Protestant Christians from Europe's Continent
      1) German pietists
      2) German and Swedish Lutherans
      3) French Huguenots
      4) Dutch Calvinists
    c. Roman Catholic Christians
      1) English (17th century) and Irish (latter 18th century)
      2) French and Spanish
    d. Portuguese Jews (including Spanish and Dutch)
  2. Subsequent immigration in significant numbers
    a. Protestant Christians
      1) Great Britain and Northern Ireland
      2) Germany, Low Countries, Scandinavia, and Baltic peoples
    b. Roman Catholic Christians
      1) Poland
      2) Italy
      3) Mexico, Cuba, and Puerto Rico
      4) Low Countries and Germany
      5) Austro-Hungarian Empire peoples
      6) French Canada
      7) Southern Ireland
    c. Eastern Orthodox Christians
      1) Greeks, Armenians, Bulgars, South Slavs
      2) Russians, Ukrainians, Finns, and Baltic peoples
    d. Jews
      1) German Jews
      2) Russian, Polish, and Baltic Jews
    e. Moslems from central and eastern Mediterranean lands
    f. Oriental faiths from China, Japan, and India

D. Protestantism
1. Diverse groups
   a. Varied origins and backgrounds
   b. Sectarianism
   c. Denominationalism and interdenominationalism
2. Fundamentalism—strongest in rural South and West
3. Liberalism or modernism
4. Church and sect memberships influenced by
   a. Social class and community status
   b. Ethnic considerations
5. Majority of Americans

E. Roman Catholicism
1. Colonial beginnings
   a. English Maryland
   b. French Louisiana
   c. Spanish Texas, New Mexico, and California
2. Large scale immigration
   a. Ireland
   b. Germany
   c. Poland
   d. Italy
   e. Austro-Hungarian Empire
3. Catholicism in the U.S.A.
   a. Endured prejudicial treatment
      1) Colonial era
      2) Irish in 19th century
   b. Strong American nationalistic currents
   c. Urban concentrations in North
   d. Recent rapid rise to full equality of opportunity
   e. Domination of church offices by Irish Americans

F. Judaism
1. Portuguese colonial, German, and Russo-Polish
2. Jewish Centers
   a. Eastern cities
   b. Certain industries and businesses
3. Doctrinal differences and ways of life
   a. Orthodox
   b. Liberal or Reform
   c. Conservative

    4. Zionism and the state of Israel

G. Secular factors in the shaping of U.S. religions
    1. Governmental or political
        a. Federalism and nationalism
        b. Democracy
        c. The Constitution
            1) Right of free belief
            2) Liberty of others to believe and worship or
               not to believe or worship
            3) Issues arise regularly
    2. Capitalism and prevailing socio-economic philoso-
       phy
    3. Science and scientism
    4. Ethnic origins and social backgrounds of the Amer-
       ican people

H. Dynamic factors molding the religious life of Americans
    1. Fundamentalism, authoritarianism, and modernism
    2. Evangelism and revivalism
    3. Puritanism
    4. Spiritualism and mysticism
    5. Secularism
    6. Overseas missions

III. DISCUSSION PROBLEMS

    1) What is meant by the term "village atheist," and
what is the rôle of atheism in the United States? Of agnos-
ticism?

    2) Is it true that Americans believe in religion in a
way that perhaps no other people do?

    3) In what respects do the various churches of the
United States, even those imported directly from Europe,
possess qualities in common?

    4) What can we understand by the verdict of one
scholar that the most substantial commitment of the
American people, to which their religiosity is instru-
mental, is the American Way of Life?

    5) Of what significance is it that, though American

denominations have developed out of sects for the greater part, they represent the final stage of development rather than a transitional stage to something more universal?

6) Of what importance have the Irish been in shaping Roman Catholicism to the major patterns of American life?

7) What is to be understood by the observation that the historical evolution of American Jewry is so characteristically American as to reveal the inner patterns of American social development?

8) If secularism is characteristic of Americans, is this not inconsistent with a sincere attachment to religion?

9) What is it, in the last analysis, that makes an American Jew strive to retain his Jewish culture?

10) Is it possible to affirm that Protestantism still defines the American religious pattern in general, to which American Catholic and American Jew will increasingly conform each in his own way and from his own direction?

11) Can it be decided after all that, wherever religion is involved, the United States is preeminently a land of minorities?

12) What religious influences outside the Judeo-Christian traditions are making headway in the United States?

IV. STUDY EXERCISES

Prepare a map of the United States to illustrate certain geographical aspects of religious distribution.

Prepare a chart for 1800, 1900, and today to illustrate the proportional strengths of America's religious groupings.

V. ADDITIONAL READINGS

E. T. Clark, *The Small Sects in America,* New York (Abingdon), 1949.

J. T. Ellis, *American Catholicism,* Chicago (University of Chicago), 1956.

N. Glazer, *American Judaism,* Chicago (University of Chicago), 1957.

O. Handlin, *The Uprooted,* Boston (Little, Brown), 1951, (Grosset and Dunlap), 1957.

W. S. Hudson, *American Protestantism,* Chicago (University of Chicago), 1961.

C. E. Olmstead, *History of Religion in the United States,* Englewood Cliffs (Prentice-Hall), 1960.

H. W. Schneider, *Religion in 20th Century America,* Cambridge (Harvard University), 1952.

The Character of the American People

II. MAJOR TOPICS: The Character of the American People

A. *The general problem for students*
   1. To determine to what degree in specific instances the general observable characteristics of the earth's nationalities are shared by individual persons
   2. To determine what are the national characteristics of the American people, and how these characteristics shape individual Americans
   3. To identify and evaluate those environmental and historical factors which help to make Americans what they are today
   4. To make illustrative comparisons between Americans and other nationals

B. The problem of national characteristics
   1. Examples of nationalities
   2. Certain attitudes, manners, and customs seem to characterize nationalities

C. The Land and the American people
   1. Review topic: The Land and Its Resources
   2. The U.S.A.
      a. Size and location
      b. Topography and resources
      c. Climates and weather
      d. Social and economic regions
      e. Solitude or isolation

3. The American people
   a. Indigenous Indians, Eskimos, Polynesians
   b. The population of the British, French, Dutch, Swedish, and Spanish colonies of North America, including Negro slaves
   c. Immigration of the 19th and 20th centuries
   d. Heterogeneous origins and folkways
4. The structures of American life
   a. The Constitution and the laws
   b. Politics and government
   c. Private property and capitalism
   d. Family and community
   e. Social class or status
   f. Heritage of slavery
   g. Judeo-Christian religions

D. The shaping of the American mind
   1. Protestantism and puritanism
   2. Rationalism and idealism
   3. Experimentalism and pragmatism
   4. Individualism, liberty, and democracy
   5. Evolution, progress, self-perfectibility, and millennialism
   6. Materialism and work
   7. Effects of the stereotyped personality
      a. Optimism, extravagance, exaggeration, and humor
      b. Lack of traditionalism or reflectiveness
      c. Impulsiveness and irresponsibility

E. Manners and folkways of Americans
   1. The English language
      a. General differences or similarities with the mother tongue
         1) Pronunciation and speech rhythms
         2) Vocabulary
         3) Meaning
      b. Dialects
      c. Non-English ingredients
      d. American literature

2. Foods and beverages
    a. National patterns
        1) General diet
        2) Average intake or consumption
        3) Schedules of eating and drinking
        4) Festive occasions
    b. Variations
        1) Regional
        2) Social class
        3) Ethnic or religious
        4) Seasonal
3. Clothing
    a. Male
    b. Female
    c. Children
4. Housing
    a. Urban
    b. Suburban
    c. Rural and small town
5. Sex, marriage, and child rearing
    a. Puberty and adolescence
    b. Courtship
    c. Equality of husband and wife
    d. The child-centered home
    e. Schooling and goals for youth
6. Miscellaneous factors of importance
    a. Personal names
    b. Recreation
    c. Holidays and vacations
    d. The arts
    e. Mass communications media
    f. The automobile
    g. Division of household labors and responsibilities
    h. Community influences and activities
    i. Health, disease, longevity, and death
    j. Abundance or poverty

F. The American character: a summary

III. DISCUSSION PROBLEMS

1) If "success" is a fundamental goal for all Americans, as it is often said to be, how can any individual American

become successful? Is his success to be equated with happiness?

2) Is it true that Americans work harder than certain other peoples? Why?

3) What contrasts, if any, do American women present to women around the globe? Is there any identifiable set of personality characteristics for America's females?

4) When, how, and in what forms do the children of the United States acquire traits of personality which are recognizably those of the American nation?

5) Which so-called "American" mannerisms or habits of action and belief might be regarded as pertaining to social class or status instead of to nationality?

6) What are some of the seeming contradictions in American life which frequently puzzle foreigners?

7) How and by what particular means is the individual American tied into the life of his community?

8) Do you think American sports emphasize the individual's rôle or team play? Why?

9) Does today's American citizen embody personality traits derived from the days of the western frontier?

10) What are the distinctive features of the American family? How does each member of the family define his or her duties and obligations?

11) Is it of any significance for understanding the character of the American people that biography is an unusually popular form of literary expression?

12) "What, then, is this new man, this American?" asked Hector St. John de Crèvecouer.

IV. STUDY EXERCISES

Prepare a "personality profile" for the American character. Then prepare another such profile for a people as nearly the same as the American's, and also for one which is approximately diametrically opposed.

V. ADDITIONAL READINGS

W. Blair, *Native American Humor,* San Francisco (Chandler), 1960.

D. W. Brogan, *The American Character,* New York (Vintage), 1956.

L. Hartz, *The Liberal Tradition in America,* New York (Harcourt, Brace), 1955.

D. M. Potter, *People of Plenty,* Chicago (University of Chicago), 1954.

C. M. Rourke, *American Humor,* New York (Doubleday Anchor), 1953.

D. Riesman, *Individualism Reconsidered,* Glencoe (Free Press), 1954.

G. Santayana, *Character and Opinion in the United States,* New York (Doubleday), 1956.

The Values of the American Nation

I. REQUIRED READINGS

    B. Smith, *Why We Behave Like Americans*, pp. 13-322.
               or
    G. R. Stewart, *American Ways of Life*, pp. 13-280.

II. MAJOR TOPICS: The Values of the American Nation

A. *The general problem for students*
1. To recognize the difficulty of defining the features and qualities of a whole nation
2. To assess the complex mixture of ideals and performances which are contained in the culture of the American people
3. To relate the outlines of American culture to the personal characteristics of individual Americans
4. To seek illustrative comparisons and contrasts between the culture of the U.S.A. and
   a. Your own national culture
   b. Different and similar national cultures

B. The national culture of the American people
1. National culture as a people's way of life
   a. Accumulated knowledge and beliefs
   b. System of values
2. The "American Way of Life" as the national culture of the U.S.A.

C. The self-image of the American nation
1. Pragmatic experimentalism and evolutionary progress
2. Law and morality
3. Republicanism, liberty, and democracy
4. Peace rather than war

5. Religion and education
6. Manifest destiny
7. Dignity of individual
8. Private ownership of property
9. Respect for labor
10. Sanctity of family life and monogamous marriage

D. Clashes between actual practice and the national self-image illustrated by
1. Racial and ethnic tensions
2. Poverty and unemployment
3. Wars and their aftermath
4. Religiosity and moralism
5. Imperial expansion and conquests
6. Education for average results
7. Crime, delinquency, alcoholism, mental illness, and ignorance
8. Social caste, class, unequal status and opportunity
9. Family upheavals and divorce

E. Habits and patterns of social organization
1. Individual responsibility
   a. Community problems
   b. Voluntarism
2. Bureaucracy
   a. Government and military services
   b. Corporate business
   c. Educational, religious, and charitable institutions
3. Individualism and the "organization man"

F. Upholding America's moral order
1. Good and evil
   a. Specific definitions and examples
   b. Conflicts between ideal goals and special interests
2. Sin and responsibility
   a. Sin and wrongdoing as individual actions
   b. Social responsibility for sin and wrongdoing
   c. Laws and reformers
   d. The churches and churchmen

3. Crime and punishment
    a. Degrees of seriousness
    b. Revenge and rehabilitation
    c. Federal-state jurisdictional conflicts
4. Death and Judeo-Christian beliefs
    a. Capital punishment
    b. Belief in an afterlife
    c. Funeral and burial customs

G. Evolution of American values in recent years
    1. Science and scientism
    2. Pragmatism and relativism
        a. Education and knowledge
        b. Indications of changing patterns of morality
            1) Parental authority
            2) Dress and behavior
            3) Juvenile delinquency
            4) Literary and artistic conventions
    3. Freudianism and the psychology of the subconscious
    4. Government and the individual
        a. Welfare-state services and disputes
        b. Resurgence of self-conscious nationalistic conservatism
    5. Contemporary America
        a. Religiosity
        b. Existentialism
        c. Nationalism
        d. Scientific attitude

H. The values of the American nation: a summary

III. DISCUSSION PROBLEMS

1) Is it to the credit of the people of America that they have not permitted a blind veneration for antiquity to overrule the suggestions of their own good sense, the knowledge of their own situation, and the lessons of their own experience?

2) Does the political life of the United States reveal fundamental insights into the ethical tone and morality of

society? Does intimate knowledge of business life tend to confirm or reject first impressions of the United States?

3) What is the place or status of the artist or intellectual in American society? Does it differ significantly from other societies?

4) In what respects is democracy dependent on religion in the United States? Does this question afford any insights into the peculiarities of American democracy?

5) How do you account for inequalities of wealth or station in the United States even though the Declaration of Independence affirms that "all men are created equal"? How do other societies compare with the United States in such respects?

6) What do you think Harold Laski might have meant when he discovered "the fallacy of abstraction" to be "a central element in Americanism"? Do Americans adhere to abstract principles more than other peoples?

7) To what extent have the values of the American nation been altered by the latterday interweaving of the welfare and garrison states?

8) Is it not paradoxical to affirm that education in the United States is not a system at all, yet belief in the importance and effectiveness of education is central to the American system?

9) What has been happening to American culture as class distinctions have become less and less visible, when the majority have leisure and money to spend?

10) Can you suggest why Susanne Langer decided of the United States that "music is our myth of the inner life"? What is jazz?

11) Is it true, as visitors complain, that Americans lack a tragic view of life? Why?

12) What can be learned of the culture and values of the American nation from its games and use of leisure?

IV. STUDY EXERCISES

Prepare a diagram of American society. Then do likewise for another national society as nearly similar to the United States as you can suggest, and also for one which is approximately diametrically opposed.

V. ADDITIONAL READINGS

R. Bendix and S. M. Lipset, *Class, Status, and Power,* Glencoe (Free Press), 1953.

J. Bryce, *The American Commonwealth,* 2 Vols. London and New York (Macmillan), 1906, New York (Putnam's Capricorn), 1959.

M. Lerner, *America as a Civilization,* New York (Simon and Schuster), 1957.

R. F. Nichols, *Religion and American Democracy,* Baton Rouge (Louisiana State University), 1959.

D. Riesman, *The Lonely Crowd,* New Haven (Yale University), 1950.

A. de Tocqueville, *Democracy in America,* 2 Vols. (1835, 1840), New York (Knopf Vintage), 1945, 1954.

M. G. White, *Social Thought in America,* Boston (Beacon), 1957.

R. M. Williams, Jr., *American Society,* New York (Knopf), 1960.

Part B: Review

LIVING IDEAS AND INSTITUTIONS

A. *The general problem for students* is to think over thoroughly and systematically what living ideas and institutions have combined to produce the present characteristics of life in the U.S.A.

B. The Federal system in principle and practice
  1. Dual nature of government in the U.S.A.
     a. Federal government
     b. Fifty state governments
  2. The separation of powers
     a. The Federal system
        1) National government
        2) State governments
     b. Checks and balances
        1) Executive powers
        2) Legislative powers
        3) Judicial powers
     c. Compromises and conflicts
  3. The Constitution of the U.S.A. (1787)
     a. Supreme law of the land
     b. Amendments
        1) Bill of Rights (1791)
        2) Amendments XI-XXIII (1798-1961)
     c. The unwritten Constitution
  4. Dual citizenship
  5. Process of Federal lawmaking, administration, and enforcement
  6. Laws and powers of the states
     a. "Sovereignty"
     b. Local governmental subdivisions

73

C. Government and politics
   1. Evolutionary developments
      a. Party system: characteristics and functions
         1) Two major parties
         2) Minor parties
      b. Spread of democracy
      c. Growth of size and power of government
   2. Voting and elective officeholding
   3. Manifestations of public opinion
   4. Today's major political parties
      a. Democrats
      b. Republicans
   5. Administration and bureaucracy
   6. Taxation

D. The place of business
   1. U.S.A. seen as a "business society"
      a. Small businesses
      b. Medium to large businesses
      c. Giant corporations
   2. Influence and prestige of businessmen
   3. Business and technological development
      a. Impact of science and technology on business
      b. Rôle of business in promoting technology
      c. Major stages of U.S. industrial development
   4. Characteristics and significance of the corporate form of business and industrial organization
      a. Historical phases of economic life
      b. The modern American corporation
         1) Ownership separated from control
         2) Dominating non-governmental element of national economy
         3) Scientific management
         4) Varying degrees of public regulation
   5. Business and the values of American society

E. Religion and the churches
   1. Historical diversification
      a. Colonial ingredients
      b. Subsequent immigration
      c. Separation of church and state

2. American Protestantism: the majority grouping
   a. Diverse groups and persuasions
   b. Sectarianism and denominationalism
   c. Doctrinal conflicts
   d. Membership and attitudes influenced by ethnic and social considerations
3. Roman Catholicism in the U.S.A.
   a. Colonial origins
   b. Aided by massive waves of immigration
   c. Present characteristics
      1) Urban and nationalistic
      2) Irish dominance
      3) Conquest of earlier discriminatory treatment
4. Judaism
5. Various Oriental faiths and followings
6. Dynamic secular forces at work

F. The character and values of the American people
   1. Individual characteristics of Americans
      a. Problem of defining national characteristics
      b. Traits which are unmistakably American, if any
      c. Necessary considerations
         1) Ethnic or cultural origins
         2) Age and sex
         3) Religious beliefs
         4) Regional and class or occupational background
      d. Shared institutions, ideas, or habits
         1) English language and legal structures
         2) Christian religion or ethics
         3) American nationalism and history
         4) Democratic individualism
         5) Education along American lines
         6) Secular social outlooks
         7) Hardworking and technologically advanced
   2. The national culture
      a. The "American Way of Life"
      b. The national self-image
      c. Conflicts between the self-image and everyday reality
      d. Habits and patterns of social organization

e. The moral order
1) Good and evil
2) Sin and responsibility
3) Crime and punishment
4) Death and belief in an after-life
f. Evolution of the nation's values
1) Science and scientism
2) Pragmatism and relativism
3) Freudianism
4) Government and the individual
5) Contemporary attitudes
3. Individual Americans as representatives of the U.S.A.: the problem of understanding

II. THE AMERICAN AND HIS NATION

Prepare a list of what might be considered as the ingredients *essential* to the making of an American, without which in any considerable degree there would be either a dissenter against the central threads of society or a citizen from another country.

Part C: Related Subjects

Science and Technology

II. MAJOR TOPICS: Science and Technology

A. *The general problem for students*
   1. To comprehend the nature and extent of the scientific revolution of recent years
   2. To assess the meaning for mankind of this revolution in control over the forces of nature
   3. To distinguish between science and technology and to determine what place each occupies in American society

B. Modern science and its impacts on human society
   1. Spectacular developments at accelerating tempos
      a. Physical sciences
      b. Biological sciences
   2. Scientific technology (applied principles of science) —some examples:
      a. Synthetic chemicals, fabrics, paints, and dyes
      b. Medicines and nutrients
      c. Chemical fertilizers and insect sprays
      d. Internal combustion engines
      e. Heating and cooling devices
      f. Aircraft and submarines
      g. Nuclear weapons and atomic-electric power plants
      h. Space vehicles
   3. Modern science and modern man
      a. Better standards of living for expanding populations

b. Perennial problem of control over man's natural environment
c. The changing appearance of fundamental truth and reality

C. The changing scientific scene: some major breakthroughs
1. Physical sciences
   a. Relativity principle
   b. Discovery of sub-atomic particles
   c. Quantum mechanics
   d. Uncertainty and probability
2. Astronomy or astro-physics
   a. Giant telescopes, photographic mapping of the heavens, and radio telescopes
   b. Speculation upon the creation and directions of the universe
3. Biological sciences (with chemistry)
   a. Conquest and control of many bacteriological and virological diseases
   b. Genetics
   c. Animal and plant nutrition
   d. Search for origins and nature of life itself
   e. Marine biology and botany
4. Psychology
   a. Heredity and environment
   b. The subconscious
   c. Psychoanalysis and psychotherapy
   d. Physiology of mental processes and diseases
5. Geology and oceanography

D. Advances in industrial technology
1. The "power" revolution
   a. Water and steam
   b. Electricity
   c. Internal combustion engines
   d. Atomic energy
2. The process of "industrial revolution"
   a. Communications and transportation networks

    b. Basic extractive and manufacturing industries
    c. Mass production and distribution
       1) Low costs
       2) Assembly-line production
       3) "Scientific" management
       4) Automation: the automatic factory
  3. Social changes
    a. Decline of proportional importance of rural population
    b. Transformation of agriculture
    c. Rise of cities and factory populations
    d. Appearance of a managerial bureaucracy

E. Science and human conduct
  1. The scientific method
    a. Hypothesis, inquiry, repeated experimentation
    b. Mathematics
  2. The social sciences
    a. Inquiry and understanding into human conduct
    b. Manipulation
  3. Scientific "truth" and cosmology
    a. Heliocentric universe—Copernicus, Kepler, Galileo
    b. Mechanistic universe—Bacon, Newton
    c. Evolving universe—Darwin
    d. Relativistic universe—Einstein
  4. Some examples of political and social thought derived from scientific views of the universe
    a. Natural law and natural rights
       1) U.S.A.—Declaration of Independence
       2) France—Declaration of the Rights of Man
    b. Science and evolution
       1) Idea of progress
       2) Karl Marx and the dialectics of historical materialism
    c. Relativism
       1) Progressive education
       2) "Modernist" theology and codes of morality or ethics
       3) Abstract art

F. Science and technology in the U.S.A.
  1. Science
      a. "Pure" or non-applied science
      b. Science in society
          1) Education
          2) Business
          3) Government
      c. The scientist
          1) Prestige and rewards
          2) Future prospects
  2. Technology
      a. Applied science
      b. The technician
          1) Education
          2) Business
          3) Government
  3. Science and public opinion

III. DISCUSSION PROBLEMS

1) Is there such a thing as the "scientific" method? If so, what exactly is it?

2) What novel relationships have arisen in recent years between society and science? Why?

3) What general distinction can be made between what occurs when advances are made in pure or theoretical science as opposed to advances made in applied science or technology?

4) Why is it that for most people the large-scale release of atomic energy accomplished since 1940 is symbolic of the new physics?

5) "The grand test of the reality of what we call matter," according to Professor P. G. Tait in 1876, "the proof that it has an objective existence, is its indestructibility and uncreatability,—if the term may be used,—by any process at the command of man." What would this statement mean to us today?

6) What are quantum mechanics? What should ordinary people understand about them and their philosophical implications?

7) Examine your own conduct for a day or two and

try to list how many decisions, made at least half consciously, are determined by the findings of scientists in the last one hundred years.

8) Is it true that if you are dealing with scientific and technical matters, judgment of values rarely, if ever, enters in?

9) Of what importance is it that scientists who scorned the technological conservatism of military men in 1940 could remark upon the almost fanatic enthusiasm for research and development of their successors of the 1950s?

10) Explain the idea that scientific theories are guides to the action of scientists which gradually become part of our common-sense ideas about the material universe.

11) Can science save man from himself? Or is technology more likely to do so?

IV. STUDY EXERCISES

Prepare a list of what you believe to be the outstanding achievements of modern science. Which of these more appropriately belong in a category for applied science or technology? Does man need more science or more technology? Explain your views.

Summarize what social circumstances seem to produce important scientific achievements. Are these the same as for achievements in philosophy, music, and the fine arts? In business and industry? In politics? In the social sciences in general?

V. ADDITIONAL READINGS

R. Brady, *Organization, Automation, and Society: the Scientific Revolution in Industry,* Berkeley (University of California), 1961.

L. Eiseley, *The Immense Journey,* New York (Random House), 1957.

G. Gamow, *One, Two, Three . . . Infinity,* New York (Viking), 1961.

B. Jaffe, *Men of Science in America,* New York (Simon and Schuster), 1958.

G. Murchie, *Music of the Spheres,* Boston (Houghton, Mifflin) 1961.

L. S. Silk, *The Research Revolution,* New York (McGraw-Hill), 1960.

V. F. Weisskopf, *Knowledge and Wonder,* New York (Doubleday), 1962.

The Industrial Society

I. REQUIRED READINGS

N. S. Buchanan and H. S. Ellis, *Approaches to Economic Development*, pp. 119-233, 406-454.

P. F. Drucker, *The Practice of Management*, pp. 1-392.

F. Peterson, *American Labor Unions*, pp. 1-330.

II. MAJOR TOPICS: The Industrial Society

A. *The general problem for students*
   1. To be familiar with the general history of industrial development in the U.S.A., and the rise of labor organizations
   2. To draw comparisons or contrasts between developments in the U.S.A. and events in other countries
   3. To account for the generally middle-class or non-proletarian qualities of the American labor movement

B. The advent of industrial conditions
   1. Economic development as recorded history
      a. Early development in England
      b. Western Europe and Europe overseas
      c. The United States of America
      d. Japan
      e. Soviet Union
      f. Elsewhere
   2. Growth of labor organizations in the U.S.A.
      a. Early workingmen's societies
      b. Trades' and crafts' unions
      c. Trends toward unity
         1) City central unions
         2) National unions
         3) Industrial unions

C. Growth of labor organizations in the U.S.A.
1. Early forms of unionization
2. Expansion with industrialization
3. National organizations
   a. Crafts' unions
   b. National Labor Union
   c. Knights of Labor
   d. Railway brotherhoods
   e. American Federation of Labor
   f. Industrial Workers of the World
   g. Congress of Industrial Organizations
   h. A.F.L.-C.I.O.
   i. Others

D. Structure and internal government of labor organizations
1. Federated organizations
2. International unions
3. Locals
4. Membership
   a. General qualifications and conditions
   b. Negro and female membership
   c. Foremen or supervisors
   d. Apprenticeship
   e. Finances and dues
5. The labor press
6. Educational activities
7. Insurance, co-operative, and benefit activities

E. Collective bargaining
1. General patterns of bargaining between labor and industry
   a. Negotiations
   b. Size of the bargains
      1) Industry-wide
      2) Local agreements
   c. The contract
   d. "Closed shop" and "open shop"
2. Labor disputes
   a. History of American strikes, lockouts, boycotts, and violence

     b. Today's pattern
       1) Strikes and the law
       2) Mediation and arbitration
   3. The government
     a. Department of Labor
     b. National (Railroad) Mediation Board
     c. National Labor Relations Act (1935)
       1) Amended (1947) by Taft-Hartley Act
       2) National Labor Relations Board
     d. Fair Labor Standards Act (1938)—as successively amended
       1) Minimum wages
       2) Maximum hours
     e. Action by states and municipal governments
   4. The labor force
     a. Union strength
     b. Areas relatively unaffected

F. American labor movements
   1. Early workingmen's associations
     a. Trades unions
     b. National Labor Union
     c. Railway brotherhoods
     d. Knights of Labor
   2. Job-conscious trades unionism: The American Federation of Labor
   3. General observations on 20th century U.S. labor movements
     a. Opportunistic
     b. Non-proletarian and non-revolutionary

G. Left-wing activity
   1. Early radicalism
     a. Agrarianism
     b. Utopianism
     c. Communitarianism
     d. Cooperative experimentalism
   2. Socialism
     a. Lassallean and Fourierite
     b. Marxist: First and Second Internationals

  c. Socialist Labor Party (1874)
  d. Socialist Party (1897, 1901)
 3. Syndicalism: The Industrial Workers of the World (1905)
 4. Communist Party (1919)

H. The present and the future of American labor organizations
 1. Unity and disunity
  a. A.F.L.-C.I.O.
  b. Major unions outside
   1) Teamsters
   2) Mine workers
   3) Others
  c. Jurisdictional disputes
 2. Future portents
  a. Technological unemployment
  b. Growing size of non-unionized labor force
   1) "White-collar" workers
   2) Technicians and specialists
  c. Higher wages and benefits; shorter hours and profit-sharing
 3. Labor's investment
  a. Union welfare funds
  b. Individual workers
 4. Changes likely in American labor movement

I. The role of management
 1. Emergence of "management" as a distinct social institution
 2. The functions of management
  a. Economic performance
  b. Making a productive enterprise out of human and material resources
  c. Managing workers and work
 3. Planning
  a. Present conditions
  b. Long-range future
 4. The challenge of automation
 5. The social responsibilities of management

III. DISCUSSION PROBLEMS

1) Explain the distinctive features of: a) the railway brotherhoods; b) Knights of Labor; c) American Federation of Labor; d) United Brotherhood of Carpenters and Joiners; e) American Railway Union; f) United Mine Workers; g) United Automobile Workers.

2) What was the reason why the American Federation of Labor survived when earlier big labor organizations failed?

3) What connections and tensions once existed in the U.S.A. between organized labor and the results of unlimited immigration?

4) Why has the American labor movement mystified outsiders, especially Europeans, indeed seemed at times not even to be a true movement of the working classes?

5) If the American labor movement possesses qualities different than classical proletarian movements, which make for acquiescence rather than overthrow of the system of capitalism, how can we account for the increasingly high living standards of workers in the U.S.A.?

6) Why did organized labor enjoy such a tremendous expansion during the 1930s and 1940s? With what results for American society and opinion?

7) In general what have been the attitudes and policies of American labor toward political action? To what degree has the labor movement been shaped as a result?

8) What has government in the U.S.A. to do with organized labor, and why?

9) What major problems today beset the American labor movement?

10) What exactly is "scientific management"? In what ways has it succeeded, and what are its shortcomings?

11) What is business management's legitimate authority, and where does its ultimate responsibility lie?

12) What is meant, with reference to business management, that the greatest opportunity for improved economic performance lies in the improvement of the effectiveness of people in their work?

IV. STUDY EXERCISES

Prepare a diagram of the population in the U.S.A. to

illustrate which segments of the people and which oc-
cupations operate largely within labor union control. On
a map of the U.S.A., show the regions of union strength
and weakness.

Prepare a diagram or diagrams to show the contractual
relationships existing between a worker and his employer.
Show the function of stewards, grievance procedures,
union locals, national unions and federations, umpires,
and the National Labor Relations Board.

V. ADDITIONAL READINGS

J. R. Commons, *et al.*, *History of Labour in the United States*, 4 Vols., New York (Macmillan), 1918-1935.

F. R. Dulles, *Labor in America: a History*, New York (Crowell), 1961.

E. C. Kirkland, *Industry Comes of Age*, New York (Holt, Rinehart, and Winston), 1961.

E. Mayo, *The Human Problems of an Industrial Civilization*, New York (Viking), 1960.

H. M. Pelling, *American Labor*, Chicago (University of Chicago), 1960.

S. Perlman, *A Theory of the Labor Movement*, New York (Kelley), 1949.

J. G. Rayback, *A History of American Labor*, New York (Macmillan), 1959.

P. Taft, *The A. F. of L. . . .* , 2 Vols., New York (Harper), 1957 and 1959.

Agriculture

I. REQUIRED READINGS

G. F. Deasy *et al., The World's Nations,* pp. 18-193, 908-911.

N. M. Blake, *A Short History of American Life,* pp. 23-41, 142-157, 448-468.

W. Miller, *A History of the United States,* pp. 277-287, 415-422.

N. S. Buchanan and H. S. Ellis, *Approaches to Economic Development,* pp. 237-266.

II. MAJOR TOPICS: Agriculture

A. *The general problem for students*
   1. To understand the colonial patterns and the historical development of agriculture in the U.S.A.
   2. To understand the place of agriculture in modern American society, its successes and also its problems

B. American farmers in a changing world
   1. American agriculture to the mid-19th century (2½ centuries of development)
      a. Self-sufficiency of the small-scale farm
      b. Plantations of the South
         1) Cotton, tobacco, sugar, rice, indigo, hemp, forest products
         2) Surpluses for sale and export
      c. Wool, milk, meats, and cereal grains being raised for sale by 1850
   2. The extended revolution in agriculture (to *ca.* 1910)
      a. Growth of farm population in sheer size
      b. Increase in farm production
         1) Mechanization and commercialization
         2) Cultivation of new lands

      c. Deepening involvement of U.S. farm products in world markets

      d. Farmers' organizations and political parties formed for protection against the reorganization of rural lives

    3. The "farm problem" since 1920

C. The expansion of American agriculture

    1. Land and land policies

      a. Enlargement of the public domain (1803-1848)

      b. Disposal of public lands

        1) Land surveys and sales

        2) Progressive liberalization of terms to Homestead Act (1862)

        3) Eventual hodge-podge of land laws

    2. Westward expansion—frontier farming

    3. The agricultural revolution (beginning in 1830s)

      a. Causes

        1) Relative scarcity of labor compared with land

        2) Inventions which affected sowing, cultivating, fertilizing, reaping, binding, transporting, processing, and storage

      b. Government aid (states and Federal)

        1) Research, experimentation, education, and demonstration

        2) U.S. Department of Agriculture (1862)

        3) Federal land grants for agricultural and mining colleges (1862)

      c. Industrial revolution

    4. The growth of farm production

      a. Northern agriculture

        1) Rapidly growing population

        2) Cash crops and farm specialization

        3) Transportation: canals, roads, railroads

        4) Cattle and hogs

      b. Slavery and plantation agriculture

        1) Single-crop specialization of staples

        2) Soil erosion, overproduction, falling prices

        3) Profitability or unprofitability of slavery

    5. Western agriculture

      a. The cattle kingdom

   c. Farm price supports and cash payments
   d. Crop insurance and loans
   e. Rural electrification and re-settlement
   f. Intensification of education and demonstrations
   g. Tax relief
   5. Diversification of southern agriculture

F. The "farm problem" today
   1. As the general public sees it
      a. Heavy annual expenditures to subsidize agriculture
      b. Accumulation and storage of enormous farm surpluses
      c. Rising food costs
   2. Increasing productivity
      a. Improved techniques
      b. Intensive use of fertilizers
      c. Mechanization and electrification
   3. Too many farms and farmers

III. DISCUSSION PROBLEMS

   1) Describe the self-sufficient farm which for a long period was characteristic of most American agriculture. Explain its disappearance.

   2) What occurred in the latter half of the 19th century to enable America's farmers to feed their nation's growing cities, and also to produce substantial surpluses for export?

   3) If in general it may be said that for a long time the primary importance of government for farmers was to make land available to them, what has come to be the relationship of government to American agriculture today?

   4) What exactly is the farm policy of the Federal government, as it has developed since the 1930s? Is this situation compatible with your understanding of the American economy?

   5) Describe the functioning of a pre-Civil War southern plantation operated by slave labor. Explain its disappearance. What system of tenancy and labor replaced slavery in the South?

6) What has been the significance for the farming population of the southern states of the following: a) underwriting of farm mortgages by the Federal government; b) rural electrification; c) soil conservation and rehabilitation; d) crop diversification; e) spread of industrialism.

7) Can you explain in political terms why America's farmers as an occupational group have become a specially subsidized segment of society?

8) Explain and describe the aftermath of the First World War that found American farmers left high and dry with output up and prices down, foreign markets shrunken, fixed costs a heavy burden.

9) Identify and evaluate those social and psychological changes of recent times which have produced major transformations for farmers and for consumers of farm products.

10) Does farming today in the U.S.A. offer career opportunities to young people? If so, with what qualifications and under what conditions?

11) Does the so-called "farm problem" in the United States appear to be a grave matter when viewed from the outside? Why or why not? What do you think the farm policy of the U.S. government ought to be?

12) In general, what comparisons or contrasts exist between the place and practices of agriculture in the U.S.A. and selected other countries?

13) What revolutionary changes in the farmers' methods of living and producing have transformed American agricultural life since 1940?

IV. STUDY EXERCISES

On outline maps of the United States, show the locations of the major agricultural regions.

Prepare a time-chart to illustrate since 1900 what have been the changes in relative importance between America's leading farm crops.

Prepare a time-chart since 1800 to illustrate what has been the proportional decline of farmers and farm workers to the total number of workers and gainfully employed persons in the U.S.A.

V. ADDITIONAL READINGS

U.S. Department of Agriculture Yearbook for 1940, *Farmers in a Changing World,* Washington (Government Printing Office), 1940.

P. W. Gates, *The Farmer's Age, 1815-1860,* New York (Holt, Rinehart, and Winston), 1960.

L. Nelson, *American Farm Life,* Cambridge (Harvard University), 1954.

F. A. Shannon, *The Farmer's Last Frontier . . . , 1860-1897,* New York (Farrar and Rinehart), 1945.

W. Slocum, *Agricultural Sociology,* New York (Harper), 1962.

International Relations

I. REQUIRED READINGS
   C. O. Lerche, Jr., *The Foreign Policy of the American People*, pp. 3-507.

II. MAJOR TOPICS: International Relations

A. *The general problem for students*
   1. To determine what are the elements of modern U.S. policy, and to what varying degrees these are being fulfilled
   2. To analyze the foreign policy of the United States, and to determine what factors of history, situation, national values, and public opinion have produced the nation's current foreign policy

B. American foreign policy
   1. National foreign policy of any state
      a. Advancement of national interests and objectives
      b. Relations with other states
   2. Policy formulation and execution in the U.S.A.
      a. The decisions
         1) President and Congress
         2) Public opinion
      b. Execution of foreign policy by President
      c. Congress
         1) Appropriations
         2) Approves appointments to offices
   3. The heritage of history
      a. Independence and isolation
      b. Great-power status, overseas penetration, and interventionism
      c. First World War
      d. Second World War
      e. Cold War

C. Making and executing American foreign policy
  1. The decision makers
    a. Executive branch of Federal government
    b. Congress and foreign policy
      1) Senate
      2) House of Representatives
  2. Public opinion in the American democracy
  3. Executing policy
    a. President
    b. Department of State
    c. Department of Defense
    d. Other agencies
  4. Treaties and Executive agreements

D. Historical stages in U.S. foreign relations
  1. Independence (1776-1815)
    a. Colonial experience and memories
    b. The Constitution
    c. Wars of the French Revolution and Napoleon
    d. Expansion by purchase
      1) Louisiana (France)
      2) Florida (Spain)
  2. Continentalism and rise to world-power status
    a. Monroe Doctrine
    b. "Manifest Destiny" and westward expansion
      1) Texas
      2) Oregon (Russia and Great Britain)
      3) California and New Mexico (Mexico)
      4) Alaska (Russia)
      5) Hawaiian Islands
      6) Philippine Islands, Puerto Rico, Cuba (Spain)
    c. Panama Canal
    d. Latin America
    e. "Open Door" in Far East
  3. First World War (1914-1918)
    a. Neutrality and intervention
    b. Treaty of Versailles and abstention from League of Nations
    c. Disarmament and isolationism
  4. Second World War (1939-1945)
    a. Neutrality and anti-Axis policies

b. Pearl Harbor to the war's end
c. United Nations
5. Cold War
   a. Disillusionment to containment
   b. Bipolarity
   c. New forces in today's world

E. Situational factors in contemporary American foreign policy
   1. The national interest
      a. Geography, population, and resources
      b. Traditions of foreign policy and popular attitudes
   2. The U.S.A. in a new world: 1945
      a. Postwar conditions
      b. United Nations
      c. Anti-colonialism and aspiring nationalisms
   3. The postwar foreign policy of the Soviet Union
      a. Early Soviet moves
      b. Soviet foreign-policy techniques
      c. U.S. perception of Soviet policy and action

F. American policy in the Cold War
   1. The pattern of American policy
      a. Causes of the Cold War
      b. Containment policy
         1) Assumptions
         2) Program
   2. The pattern applied
   3. The Cold War and containment
      a. Europe
         1) Truman Doctrine and Marshall Plan
         2) N.A.T.O.
      b. China (1949) and Taiwan
   4. Korean War (1950-1953)
   5. Indo-China
      a. Withdrawal of France
      b. Viet-Nam, Cambodia, Laos, and Viet-Minh
   6. Middle East
   7. Evolution of bipolarity

G. Continuing issues in American foreign policy
1. Political issues
   a. Soviet Union
   b. China
   c. Relations with allies
   d. United Nations
   e. New states and anti-colonialism
2. Military issues
   a. Overseas bases and defense commitments
   b. Arms race and weapons testing
   c. Disarmament or arms limitation
   d. Space vehicles
3. Economic issues
   a. Aid programs and military spending
   b. Trade, tariff, and exchange problems
4. Psychological issues
   a. Cold War ideological conflicts
   b. The image of the U.S.A. in other countries
5. Repercussions of foregoing issues in domestic public opinion

III. DISCUSSION PROBLEMS

1) What was the original purpose of the Monroe Doctrine of 1823? How and why has it evolved to present circumstances?

2) What relationships existed in the Orient among the great powers by 1910? To what degree and for what reasons was the United States involved?

3) What relationships existed between the United States and Latin America by 1914? How and for what reasons had these developed? What developments have followed from then until now?

4) What in a general sense were the results for the world of the First World War? What were the results for the United States and its foreign policy? How clearly were these understood by the American people?

5) Is it true, that of all the steps taken toward disarmament during the 1920s, the naval limitations ratio was at once the most decisive and the least effective?

6) What new circumstances at the end of the Second World War posed wholly new problems for the makers

of American foreign policy? What domestic repercussions occurred as a result?

7) What are the basic assumptions on which the American people have traditionally approached their foreign policy? Have these changed importantly since 1945?

8) What impact does public opinion have today on the making and carrying out of U.S. foreign policy? What are the strengths and weaknesses of American public opinion?

9) What do you understand to be the kind of world in which Americans would like to live? Is their foreign policy suitable for such a goal? Is the world headed in such a direction?

10) At what point around 1945, and for what reasons, did cooperation between the U.S.A. and the Soviet Union turn into the antagonism and rivalry which underlies the Cold War?

11) What is meant by the argument that the greatest weakness of recent American foreign policy has been its fixation on the problem of Russia?

12) Can we reach any tentative conclusions about the relative success of the U.S.A. and the Soviet Union in the struggle for the minds and hopes of mankind? Or is this not really the central question for the future?

IV. STUDY EXERCISES

Prepare diagrams to illustrate the steps by which foreign policy is made and executed by the U.S.A., and show what domestic pressures and influences can be brought to bear on foreign affairs.

On maps of the world indicate what were the major foreign policies and involvements of the U.S.A. for 1900, 1918, 1940, 1945, and 1960. Be able to explain these circumstances, and any changes since 1960.

V. ADDITIONAL READINGS

T. A. Bailey, *A Diplomatic History of the American People,* New York (Appleton-Century-Crofts), 1958.

N. M. Blake and O. T. Barck, Jr., *The United States in Its World Relations,* New York (McGraw-Hill), 1960.

J. Davids, *America and the World of Our Time,* New York (Random House), 1960.

H. W. Gatzke, *The Present in Perspective,* New York (Rand McNally), 1961.

G. F. Kennan, *American Diplomacy, 1900-1950,* Chicago (University of Chicago), 1951.

S. D. Kertesz, ed., *American Diplomacy in a New Era,* South Bend (University of Notre Dame), 1961.

J. A. Pratt, *A History of United States Foreign Policy,* Englewood Cliffs (Prentice-Hall), 1955.

Education

I. REQUIRED READINGS

J. Dewey, *The Child and the Curriculum,* pp. 7-40.
J. Dewey, *The School and Society,* pp. 3-164.
R. M. Williams, Jr., *American Society,* pp. 265-303.

II. MAJOR TOPICS: Education

A. *The general problem for students*
   1. To identify those historic forces which have shaped the American people's insistence on universal education
   2. To understand how the American educational process is organized, and how it actually functions
   3. To examine the major philosophic foundations of education in the U.S.A.

B. The general characteristics of American education
   1. The schools
      a. Institutional types
         1) Schools supported and supervised by the states
         2) Private secular schools
         3) Church-supported and -directed schools
      b. Characteristics
         1) Secular education
         2) Compulsory attendance
         3) Common cultural standards and normative patterns
         4) No central educational authority
   2. Higher education
      a. Support
         1) Private endowments and fees
         2) Appropriations by state governments or their subdivisions and fees
      b. Enormous diversity in quality and courses of study

103

C. Historic influences in the rise of universal public schooling
1. Protestantism's emphasis on literacy for bible reading
2. Political democracy and universal suffrage
3. Popular pressures for economic and social advancement
4. The needs of business and industry for technicians and clerks
5. "Americanization" of foreign-born persons

D. Organization, control, and conditions
1. States and local governments
   a. Set and enforce standards for all schools
   b. Support schools by public taxation, mainly on real estate
   c. Operate systems of public schools
2. Schools and the pupils
   a. Stages
      1) Elementary school beginning with kindergarten and continuing with grades 1-6
      2) Junior high school for grades 7-9
      3) Senior high school for grades 10-12
   b. Progression upward through the grades usually unbroken by selective examinations
   c. "Grading" system gives quantitative scores for standardized competitive achievements
3. Curriculum reflects ambivalence of public opinion and changing fads and fashions of educational philosophy
   a. Democratic and patriotic values
   b. Emphasis on practical usefulness rather than theoretical goals
4. Teachers lower in prestige and income than other professions and other countries
   a. Educational training of American teachers
   b. Teachers are mostly females at elementary and secondary levels
   c. Current trends lie in direction of improved income and training

E. Philosophic and cultural influences which have shaped or are shaping U.S. education
1. Social, political, and economic
    a. Protestantism
    b. Democracy
    c. Opportunities for trained and literate persons
2. Educational philosophies and goals represented in curricula or courses of study
    a. Technical training in vocational skills
    b. "Classical" education—moral philosophy, political economy, rhetoric, logic, algebra and geometry, Greek and Latin
    c. Pragmatism and the "life-adjustment" philosophy of "progressive education"
        1) Democratic and "practical"
        2) Elective courses
        3) Emphasis on interpersonal relations and conformity to group standards of behavior
        4) Goal: growth of the whole child
    d. Current indications and directions
        1) Differentiation by motivation and intelligence
        2) Novel emphasis on the "bright" child
        3) Heavier work loads and more exacting courses of study
        4) Greater stress on natural sciences, mathematics, and foreign languages
        5) More subject matter emphasized in teacher training as opposed to philosophy and methods of education
        6) Growing public insistence on higher educational opportunities for more students
F. Higher education
1. Colleges, universities, and professional-training institutions
2. Financial support and regulation or supervision
    a. Can be private or public or a mixture of the two
    b. State and local governments
3. Distinctive features of higher education in the U.S.A.
    a. Great diversity in quality of institutions

b. Mass enrollment and comparatively easy entrance standards

c. Successful completion of course requirements leads to degrees at the undergraduate college level

d. Campus social life and spectator sports

e. Importance of "practical" subjects and vocational courses of study

f. Ambivalent public attitudes toward intellectuals and toward subjects or books deemed impractical or threatening to group mores

g. Excellence of professional schools and institutes of graduate-study

h. Tremendous expansion currently underway in all directions

III. DISCUSSION PROBLEMS

1) Which direction ought a school curriculum to take —the teaching of the subject matter, or the teaching of the child?

2) Explain the fundamental propositions of John Dewey and his disciples. What philosophical postulates underlay "progressive education" in the U.S.A.?

3) What have been the general results for Americans of the influence of John Dewey and his disciples?

4) What is to be understood by the dogma that education should liberate "the life-process for its own most adequate fulfillment"?

5) Can you connect current trends in educational philosophy and activity, in the U.S.A. and other countries as well, with the world's general historic directions?

6) How can there be introduced into the school curriculum something to represent the demands and realities of adult life? What has the U.S. experience shown here?

7) Who goes to colleges and universities in the U.S.A.? Why? Who should go?

8) How can the astonishing range of quality in American higher education be explained? Of what importance is it that there exists this range?

9) In the U.S.A. and compared to other countries, what is the general status and condition of school pupils?

College or university students? School teachers? Professors? Explain.

10) If education in American schools is a public matter and compulsory by law, what must be explained about the church-maintained and other private schools?

11) Why can it be said that higher education in the U.S.A. presents a complex picture of public and private activity?

IV. STUDY EXERCISES

As closely as possible, compare and contrast the educational opportunities and customs of Americans with conditions found in other countries. Distinguish differences of: a) philosophy; b) finances, organization, or institutional structures; c) school, college, and professional-training courses of study; d) proportionate accessibility to educational opportunities and careers depending on training and education; e) other useful points of comparison.

V. ADDITIONAL READINGS

L. A. Cremin, *The Transformation of the School*, New York (Knopf), 1961.

"Education and American History," special issue of the *Harvard Educational Review*, Vol. XXXI (Spring 1961).

R. Hofstadter and W. P. Metzger, *The Development of Academic Freedom in the United States*, New York (Columbia University), 1955.

M. Mayer, *The Schools*, New York (Harper), 1961.

F. Rudolph, *The American College and University*, New York (Knopf), 1962.

P. Woodring, *A Fourth of a Nation*, New York (McGraw-Hill), 1957.

Regionalism in American Life

II. MAJOR TOPICS: Regionalism in American Life

A. *The general problem for students*
   1. To apply your knowledge of the geography and history of the U.S.A. to explain the emergence of distinct regions within the nation
   2. To isolate those social, economic, political, and psychological factors typical of any particular region
   3. To assess the general place of regionalism in American life, its strengths and contributions on the one hand or its futilities and self-defeating characteristics on the other

B. America's regions and regionalisms
   1. The distinctive regions of the U.S.A. today
      a. Northeast
      b. South
      c. Middle West
      d. Southwest
      e. Far West
      f. Alaska
      g. Hawaiian Islands
      h. Puerto Rico
      i. Insular territories
   2. Regionalism (localism or particularism)
      a. Geography and history
      b. Psychological self-consciousness, even separatism
         1) Dialect, diet, custom, social code

108

2) Literature, art, architecture, songs or dances, and recreations
3) Rudimentary nationalism or consciousness of kind

C. The northeastern region
   1. New England and the Mid-Atlantic states
      a. Originally two or more distinct regions
      b. Urban, industrial, and commercial
         1) High population density
         2) Dairying, fruit and vegetable farming to supply cities
      c. Sharp seasonal variations of climate
   2. Regionalism
      a. Scattered remnants of older distinctions of speech patterns, diets, humor, architecture, and provincial outlooks
      b. Speech
         1) Broad "A" and nasal twang
         2) Differences according to social class are greater within the East than between the East and other sections
      c. Political slant tends toward internationalism

D. The southern region
   1. Eastern Maryland to Florida and to Arkansas and Texas
      a. Mild to sub-tropical climate
      b. Rural ways of life throughout much of southern region's history
         1) Staple crops
         2) History of slavery until 1865 and farm tenancy until recently
         3) Many geographical sub-regions and ways of life
   2. Regionalism
      a. Speech peculiarities of inflection, idiom, and drawl
      b. Diet
      c. Important features of southernism
         1) White supremacy

        2) Class cleavage between whites
        3) Conservative and traditional folkways
        4) Heritage of the Civil War

E. The middle western region
  1. Area of Ohio Valley, Great Lakes, upper Mississippi Valley, and northern Great Plains
    a. Sharp, even violent, seasonal variations of climate
    b. Generally flat topography
    c. Heartland of North America
      1) Great concentrations of heavy industry
      2) Grain and meat producing centers
  2. Regionalism
    a. Scattered remnants of older variants introduced by eastern, southern, and European origins of settlers
    b. Speech tends toward flatness with compromises between extremes of American idioms and inflections
    c. Formerly the center of political isolationism

F. The southwestern and far western regions
  1. Deserts, high mountains, plateaus, fertile slopes and valleys
    a. Generally mild to hot, arid climate, with intrusive extremes of a violent nature in mountains and southern Great Plains
    b. Important sub-regional distinctions
      1) Rocky Mountains, Sierra Nevadas, Pacific Coastal ranges
      2) Deserts and arid plateaus
      3) Littorals of Gulf of Mexico and Pacific Ocean coasts
  2. Regionalism
    a. Scattered remnants of Spanish heritage
    b. Flourishing pockets or centers of Mormon, Indian, Mexican, and Oriental life, ranching, lumbering, mining, and farming especially fruit- and vegetable-growing

    c. Nasal drawl and exaggerated idioms of western speech; extravagance of humor

    d. Spectacular growth and influence of Texas and California as focal points of western life and changing ways

    e. Tendency for distinctive flavors (speech, diet, custom, etc.) to be overwhelmed by

       1) Population growth

       2) Industrialization and nationalization of cultural patterns

  3. The West as romantic myth and contemporary reality

G. The separated portions of the United States as distinctive regions

  1. Alaska

  2. Hawaiian Islands

  3. Puerto Rico and the insular territories

H. Regionalism and the nation's cultural trends: a summary and evaluation

III. DISCUSSION PROBLEMS

    1) In an overall picture of American life, what importance would you assign to regionalism? Why?

    2) Even if you have never visited the separate regions of the United States, do you think you can identify the regional origins of Americans when you meet them?

    3) Where have geographic factors been most important in defining America's regionalism? Historic factors? Social factors?

    4) In what instances today, and to what extent, do regional differences affect national politics in the U.S.A.? With what important results if any?

    5) What significant regional manifestations, if any, have worked to shape the arts in the U.S.A., including literature, architecture, sculpture, painting, music, and the dance?

    6) What observations can be made about the English language in the U.S.A., in terms of regional similarities

or differences? Can you compare your conclusions with
what you know of the situation in Great Britain?

7) Historically speaking, have the regions of the
U.S.A. always been identical with today's?

8) Why is it necessary to consider Alaska, the Hawaiian Islands, and Puerto Rico as distinct and separate
regions within the U.S.A.? What are the special qualities
of each?

9) Can you conveniently summarize some important
regional variations of American dietary habits? Are these
of superficial or basic importance?

10) How influential have settlements of immigrants
been in creating regional differences within the U.S.A.?

11) What trends or conditions within today's U.S.A.
seem to be transforming regionalism as a factor in American life?

IV. STUDY EXERCISES

Compare regionalism in American life with manifestations of localism, provincialism, or particularism in a number of other countries. In addition to geography and history, include considerations of religious, linguistic, and
ethnic differences, dietary and dress customs, folkways,
dialects and speech patterns, architecture, the arts, and
popular diversions. Did you discover any regionalism
similar to any found in the United States?

V. ADDITIONAL READINGS

L. E. Atherton, *Main Street on the Middle Border*,
Bloomington (Indiana University), 1954.

R. A. Billington, *The Far Western Frontier*, New York
(Harper), 1956.

R. A. Billington, *The Westward Movement in the
United States*, Princeton (Van Nostrand Anvil), 1959.

W. J. Cash, *The Mind of the South*, New York (Knopf),
1941 and New York (Vintage), 1960.

R. M. Dorson, *American Folklore*, Chicago (University
of Chicago), 1959.

A. Kazin, *A Walker in the City*, New York (Grove),
1958.

C. F. Kraenzel, *The Great Plains in Transition,* Norman (University of Oklahoma), 1955.

E. S. Osgood, *The Day of the Cattleman,* Chicago (University of Chicago), 1957.

F. B. Simkins, *A History of the South,* New York (Knopf), 1953.

L. B. Wright, *Culture on the Moving Frontier,* Bloomington (Indiana University), 1955.

Part C: Review

A. *The general problem for students* is to think over thoroughly and systematically which special topics can provide deeper insights into the life and thought and institutions of the American people, and also supply valuable points of comparison and contrast with other peoples elsewhere.

B. Science and technology
  1. Modern science and its impacts on human society
    a. Spectacular and rapid development
    b. Applied science and technology
    c. Relationships between science and man
    d. The changing appearance of fundamental truth and reality
  2. The contemporary scientific scene
    a. Physical sciences
    b. Biological sciences
    c. Behavioral sciences
  3. Science and technology in the U.S.A.

C. The industrial society
  1. Spread of industrial conditions
    a. Beginnings in England and on the continent of Europe
    b. The United States of America
    c. Industrializing the earth's peoples
  2. Growth and structure of labor organizations in the U.S.A.
    a. Expansion with industrialization
    b. National organizations
    c. Structure and internal government

115

        d. Collective bargaining
        e. History of industrial disputes and violence
    3. The government
        a. Early opposition to associations of workingmen
        b. Change to public sympathy and support for organized labor
           1) Maintenance of minimum standards
           2) Mediation and conciliation services
    4. American labor's relationships to left-wing politics
        a. Utopianism
        b. Trades unionism
        c. Socialism
        d. Syndicalism and communism
        e. General characteristics of U.S. labor
           1) Opportunistic
           2) Non-revolutionary
    5. The prospects for change in the years ahead

  D. Agriculture
    1. American farmers in a changing world
        a. To mid-19th century
        b. The extended revolution in U.S. agriculture
           1) Increase of acreage under cultivation and growth of farm population
           2) Per capita increase in production
           3) Involvement in world markets
           4) Governmental protection
           5) Continuous advances of scientific agriculture
    2. Agrarian unrest of the late 19th century
        a. Farmers' organizations
        b. Ended by prosperity and stability
    3. American agriculture in recent years
        a. Cooperative marketing organizations
        b. Lengthy depression after 1920
        c. Effects of social and technological changes
        d. Federal government's support and assistance
        e. The permanent "farm problem"

  E. International relations
    1. Making and executing U.S. foreign policy
        a. The decision-makers

  b. Public opinion
  c. The Office of the President
 2. Historical stages in U.S. foreign relations
  a. Winning and guaranteeing independence
  b. Expansion to world-power status
  c. First World War
  d. Second World War
  e. Cold War
 3. American policy in the Cold War
  a. Policy of containment
  b. Containment applied
   1) Europe
   2) China
   3) Korea
   4) Indo-China
   5) Middle East
  c. Evolution of bipolarity
  d. Support for the United Nations

F. Education
 1. The general characteristics of American education
  a. Schools
  b. Colleges and universities
 2. Historic factors contributing to universal public schooling
  a. Protestantism
  b. Democracy
  c. Individualism and opportunism
  d. Needs of business and industry
  e. "Americanization"
 3. Institutional structure and controls
  a. States and local governments
  b. Pupils and the curriculum
 4. Philosophic and cultural pressures on U.S. education
  a. Social, political, and economic attitudes
  b. Educational philosophies
   1) Vocational training
   2) "Classical" learning
   3) "Progressive education"
   4) Contemporary trends

    5. Higher education
      a. Public and private blend
      b. Tremendous range of quality, offerings, and opportunities
      c. Expansion

II. THE VARIETY OF APPROACHES TO AMERICAN LIFE

Choose any single approach to the study of the American people and the U.S.A., either from among the topics of this *Syllabus* or another of your own preference, which you can defend as the most instructive and illuminating of all points of view. Then write a short essay of explanation and illustration.

Documents and Maps

The Declaration of Independence, *1776*

In Congress, July 4, 1776
The unanimous Declaration of the thirteen
United States of America

When in the course of human events, it becomes necessary for one people to dissolve the political bands which have connected them with another, and to assume among the powers of the earth, the separate and equal station to which the Laws of Nature and of Nature's God entitle them, a decent respect to the opinions of mankind requires that they should declare the causes which impel them to the separation.

We hold these truths to be self-evident, that all men are created equal, that they are endowed by their Creator with certain unalienable rights, that among these are life, liberty and the pursuit of happiness. That to secure these rights, governments are instituted among men, deriving their just powers from the consent of the governed. That whenever any form of government becomes destructive of these ends, it is the right of the people to alter or to abolish it, and to institute new government, laying its foundation on such principles and organizing its powers in such form, as to them shall seem most likely to effect their safety and happiness. Prudence, indeed, will dictate that governments long established should not be changed for light and transient causes; and accordingly all experience hath shown, that mankind are more disposed to suffer, while evils are sufferable, than to right themselves by abolishing the forms to which they are accustomed. But when a long train of abuses and usurpations, pursuing invariably the same object evinces a design to reduce them under absolute despotism, it is their right, it is their duty, to throw off such government, and to provide new guards for their future security. Such has been the patient sufferance of these Colonies; and such is now the necessity which constrains them to alter their former systems of government. The history of the present King of Great Britain is a history of repeated injuries and usurpations, all having in direct object the establishment of an absolute tyranny over these States. To prove this, let facts be submitted to a candid world.

He has refused his assent to laws, the most wholesome and necessary for the public good.

He has forbidden his Governors to pass laws of immediate and pressing importance, unless suspended in their operation till his assent should be obtained; and when so suspended, he has utterly neglected to attend to them.

He has refused to pass other laws for the accommodation of large districts of people, unless those people would relinquish the right of representation in the Legislature, a right inestimable to them and formidable to tyrants only.

He has called together legislative bodies at places unusual, uncomfortable, and distant from the depository of their public records, for the sole purpose of fatiguing them into compliance with his measures.

He has dissolved representative houses repeatedly, for opposing with manly firmness his invasions on the rights of the people.

He has refused for a long time, after such dissolutions, to cause others to be elected; whereby the legislative powers, incapable of annihilation, have returned to the people at large for their exercise; the State remaining in the meantime exposed to all the dangers of invasion from without and convulsions within.

He has endeavoured to prevent the population of these states; for that purpose obstructing the laws of naturalization of foreigners; refusing to pass others to encourage their migration hither, and raising the conditions of new appropriations of lands.

He has obstructed the administration of justice, by refusing his assent to laws for establishing judiciary powers.

He has made judges dependent on his will alone, for the tenure of their offices, and the amount and payment of their salaries.

He has erected a multitude of new offices, and sent hither

swarms of officers to harass our people, and eat out their substance.

He has kept among us, in times of peace, standing armies without the consent of our legislatures.

He has affected to render the military independent of and superior to the civil power.

He has combined with others to subject us to a jurisdiction foreign to our constitution, and unacknowledged by our laws; giving his assent to their acts of pretended legislation:

For quartering large bodies of armed troops among us:

For protecting them, by a mock trial, from punishment for any murders which they should commit on the inhabitants of these States:

For cutting off our trade with all parts of the world:

For imposing taxes on us without our consent:

For depriving us in many cases, of the benefits of trial by jury:

For transporting us beyond seas to be tried for pretended offences:

For abolishing the free system of English laws in a neighbouring Province, establishing therein an arbitrary government, and enlarging its boundaries so as to render it at once an example and fit instrument for introducing the same absolute rule into these Colonies:

For taking away our Charters, abolishing our most valuable laws, and altering fundamentally the forms of our governments:

For suspending our own Legislatures, and declaring themselves invested with power to legislate for us in all cases whatsoever.

He has abdicated government here, by declaring us out of his protection and waging war against us.

He has plundered our seas, ravaged our coasts, burnt our towns, and destroyed the lives of our people.

He is at this time transporting large armies of foreign mercenaries to complete the works of death, desolation and tyranny, already begun with circumstances of cruelty and perfidy scarcely paralleled in the most barbarous ages, and totally unworthy the head of a civilized nation.

He has constrained our fellow citizens taken captive on the

high seas to bear arms against their country, to become the executioners of their friends and brethren, or to fall themselves by their hands.

He has excited domestic insurrections amongst us, and has endeavoured to bring on the inhabitants of our frontiers, the merciless Indian savages, whose known rule of warfare, is an undistinguished destruction of all ages, sexes, and conditions.

In every stage of these oppressions we have petitioned for redress in the most humble terms: our repeated petitions have been answered only by repeated injury. A prince whose character is thus marked by every act which may define a tyrant is unfit to be the ruler of a free people.

Nor have we been wanting in attention to our British brethren. We have warned them from time to time of attempts by their legislature to extend an unwarrantable jurisdiction over us. We have reminded them of the circumstances of our emigration and settlement here. We have appealed to their native justice and magnanimity, and we have conjured them by the ties of our common kindred to disavow these usurpations, which would inevitably interrupt our connections and correspondence. They too have been deaf to the voice of justice and of consanguinity. We must, therefore, acquiesce in the necessity, which denounces our separation, and hold them, as we hold the rest of mankind, enemies in war, in peace friends.

We, therefore, the Representatives of the United States of America, in General Congress assembled, appealing to the Supreme Judge of the world for the rectitude of our intentions, do, in the name, and by authority of the good people of these Colonies, solemnly publish and declare, That these United Colonies are, and of right, ought to be Free and Independent States; that they are absolved from all allegiance to the British Crown, and that all political connection between them and the State of Great Britain, is and ought to be totally dissolved; and that as Free and Independent States, they have full power to levy war, conclude peace, contract alliances, establish commerce, and to do all other acts and things which Independent States may of right do. And for the support of this declaration, with a firm reliance on the protection of Divine Providence, we mutually pledge to each other our lives, our fortunes, and our sacred honor.

JOHN HANCOCK.

New Hampshire
  JOSIAH BARTLETT,
  WM. WHIPPLE,
  MATTHEW THORNTON.
Massachusetts Bay
  SAML. ADAMS,
  JOHN ADAMS,
  ROBT. TREAT PAINE,
  ELBRIDGE GERRY.
Rhode Island
  STEP. HOPKINS,
  WILLIAM ELLERY.
Connecticut
  ROGER SHERMAN,
  SAM'EL HUNTINGTON,
  WM. WILLIAMS,
  OLIVER WOLCOTT.
Georgia
  BUTTON GWINNETT,
  LYMAN HALL,
  GEO. WALTON.
Pennsylvania
  ROBT. MORRIS,
  BENJAMIN RUSH,
  BENJA. FRANKLIN,
  JOHN MORTON,
  GEO. CLYMER,
  JAS. SMITH,
  GEO. TAYLOR,
  JAMES WILSON,
  GEO. ROSS.
Delaware
  CAESAR RODNEY,
  GEO. READ,
  THO. M'KEAN.

Maryland
  SAMUEL CHASE,
  WM. PACA,
  THOS. STONE,
  CHARLES CARROLL of
    Carrollton.
Virginia
  GEORGE WYTHE,
  RICHARD HENRY LEE,
  TH. JEFFERSON,
  BENJA. HARRISON,
  THS. NELSON, JR.,
  FRANCIS LIGHTFOOT LEE,
  CARTER BRAXTON.
New York
  WM. FLOYD,
  PHIL. LIVINGSTON,
  FRANS. LEWIS,
  LEWIS MORRIS.
North Carolina
  WM. HOOPER,
  JOSEPH HEWES,
  JOHN PENN.
South Carolina
  EDWARD RUTLEDGE,
  THOS. HEYWARD, JUNR.,
  THOMAS LYNCH, JUNR.,
  ARTHUR MIDDLETON.
New Jersey
  RICHD. STOCKTON,
  JNO. WITHERSPOON,
  FRAS. HOPKINSON,
  JOHN HART,
  ABRA. CLARK.

The Constitution of the United States, *1787*

We the People of the United States, in order to form a more perfect union, establish justice, insure domestic tranquility, provide for the common defence, promote the general welfare, and secure the blessings of liberty to ourselves and our posterity, do ordain and establish this Constitution for the United States of America.

ARTICLE I

Sec. 1. All legislative powers herein granted shall be vested in a Congress of the United States, which shall consist of a Senate and House of Representatives.

Sec. 2. The House of Representatives shall be composed of members chosen every second year by the people of the several States, and the electors in each State shall have the qualifications requisite for electors of the most numerous branch of the State legislature.

No person shall be a Representative who shall not have attained to the age of twenty-five years, and been seven years a citizen of the United States, and who shall not, when elected, be an inhabitant of that State in which he shall be chosen.

Representatives and direct taxes shall be apportioned among the several States which may be included within this Union, according to their respective numbers, which shall be determined by adding to the whole number of free persons, including those bound to service for a term of years, and excluding Indians not taxed, three-fifths of all other persons. The actual enumeration shall be made within three years after the first meeting of the Congress of the United States, and within every subsequent term of ten years, in such manner as they shall by law direct. The number of Representatives shall not exceed one for every thirty thousand, but each State shall have at least one Representative; and until such enumeration shall be made, the State of New Hampshire shall be entitled to choose three,

Massachusetts eight, Rhode Island and Providence Plantations one, Connecticut five, New York six, New Jersey four, Pennsylvania eight, Delaware one, Maryland six, Virginia ten, North Carolina five, South Carolina five, and Georgia three.

When vacancies happen in the representation from any State, the executive authority thereof shall issue writs of election to fill such vacancies.

The House of Representatives shall choose their Speaker and other officers; and shall have the sole power of impeachment.

Sec. 3. The Senate of the United States shall be composed of two Senators from each State, chosen by the legislature thereof, for six years; and each Senator shall have one vote.

Immediately after they shall be assembled in consequence of the first election, they shall be divided as equally as may be into three classes. The seats of the Senators of the first class shall be vacated at the expiration of the second year, of the second class at the expiration of the fourth year, and of the third class at the expiration of the sixth year, so that one-third may be chosen every second year; and if vacancies happen by resignation, or otherwise, during the recess of the legislature of any State, the executive thereof may make temporary appointments until the next meeting of the legislature, which shall then fill such vacancies.

No person shall be a Senator who shall not have attained to the age of thirty years, and been nine years a citizen of the United States, and who shall not, when elected, be an inhabitant of that State for which he shall be chosen.

The Vice-President of the United States shall be President of the Senate, but shall have no vote, unless they be equally divided.

The Senate shall choose their other officers, and also a President pro tempore, in the absence of the Vice-President, or when he shall exercise the office of President of the United States.

The Senate shall have the sole power to try all impeachments. When sitting for that purpose, they shall be on oath or affirmation. When the President of the United States is tried, the Chief Justice shall preside: and no person shall be convicted without the concurrence of two-thirds of the members present.

Judgment in cases of impeachment shall not extend further than to removal from office, and disqualification to hold and enjoy any office of honor, trust or profit under the United States: but the party convicted shall nevertheless be liable and subject to indictment, trial, judgment, and punishment, according to law.

Sec. 4. The times, places and manner of holding elections for Senators and Representatives, shall be prescribed in each State by the legislature thereof; but the Congress may at any time by law make or alter such regulations, except as to the places of choosing Senators.

The Congress shall assemble at least once in every year, and such meeting shall be on the first Monday in December, unless they shall by law appoint a different day.

Sec. 5. Each house shall be the judge of the elections, returns and qualifications of its own members, and a majority of each shall constitute a quorum to do business; but a smaller number may adjourn from day to day, and may be authorized to compel the attendance of absent members, in such manner, and under such penalties as each house may provide.

Each house may determine the rules of its proceedings, punish its members for disorderly behaviour, and, with the concurrence of two-thirds, expel a member.

Each house shall keep a journal of its proceedings, and from time to time publish the same, excepting such parts as may in their judgment require secrecy; and the yeas and nays of the members of either house on any question shall, at the desire of one-fifth of those present, be entered on the journal.

Neither house, during the session of Congress, shall, without the consent of the other, adjourn for more than three days, nor to any other place than that in which the two houses shall be sitting.

Sec. 6. The Senators and Representatives shall receive a compensation for their services, to be ascertained by law, and paid out of the Treasury of the United States. They shall in all cases, except treason, felony and breach of the peace, be privileged from arrest during their attendance at the session of their respective Houses, and in going to and returning from the same; and for any speech or debate in either house, they shall not be questioned in any other place.

No Senator or Representative shall, during the time for which he was elected, be appointed to any civil office under the authority of the United States which shall have been created, or the emoluments whereof shall have been increased during such time; and no person holding any office under the United States, shall be a member of either House during his continuance in office.

Sec. 7. All bills for raising revenue shall originate in the House of Representatives; but the Senate may propose or concur with amendments as on other bills.

Every bill which shall have passed the House of Representatives and the Senate, shall, before it become a law, be presented to the President of the United States; if he approve he shall sign it, but if not he shall return it, with his objections to that house in which it shall have originated, who shall enter the objections at large on their journal, and proceed to reconsider it. If after such reconsideration two-thirds of that house shall agree to pass the bill, it shall be sent, together with the objections, to the other house, by which it shall likewise be reconsidered, and if approved by two-thirds of that house, it shall become a law. But in all such cases the votes of both houses shall be determined by yeas and nays, and the names of the persons voting for and against the bill shall be entered on the journal of each house respectively. If any bill shall not be returned by the President within ten days (Sundays excepted) after it shall have been presented to him, the same shall be a law, in like manner as if he had signed it, unless the Congress by their adjournment prevent its return, in which case it shall not be a law.

Every order, resolution, or vote to which the concurrence of the Senate and House of Representatives may be necessary (except on a question of adjournment) shall be presented to the President of the United States; and before the same shall take effect, shall be approved by him, or being disapproved by him, shall be repassed by two-thirds of the Senate and House of Representatives, according to the rules and limitations prescribed in the case of a bill.

Sec. 8. The Congress shall have power to lay and collect taxes, duties, imposts, and excises, to pay the debts and provide for the common defence and general welfare of the United States; but all duties, imposts, and excises shall be uniform throughout the United States;

To borrow money on the credit of the United States;

To regulate commerce with foreign nations, and among the several States, and with the Indian tribes;

To establish a uniform rule of naturalization, and uniform laws on the subject of bankruptcies throughout the United States;

To coin money, regulate the value thereof, and of foreign coin, and fix the standard of weights and measures;

To provide for the punishment of counterfeiting the securities and current coin of the United States;

To establish post-offices and post-roads;

To promote the progress of science and useful arts, by securing for limited times to authors and inventors the exclusive right to their respective writings and discoveries;

To constitute tribunals inferior to the Supreme Court;

To define and punish piracies and felonies committed on the high seas, and offences against the law of nations;

To declare war, grant letters of marque and reprisal, and make rules concerning captures on land and water;

To raise and support armies, but no appropriation of money to that use shall be for a longer term than two years;

To provide and maintain a navy;

To make rules for the government and regulation of the land and naval forces;

To provide for calling forth the militia to execute the laws of the Union, suppress insurrections and repel invasions;

To provide for organizing, arming, and disciplining the militia, and for governing such part of them as may be employed in the service of the United States, reserving to the States respectively the appointment of the officers, and the authority of training the militia according to the discipline prescribed by Congress;

To exercise exclusive legislation in all cases whatsoever, over such district (not exceeding ten miles square) as may, by cession of particular States, and the acceptance of Congress, become the seat of the Government of the United States, and to exercise like authority over all places purchased by the consent of the legislature of the state in which the same shall be, for the erection of forts, magazines, arsenals, dockyards, and other needful buildings; and

To make all laws which shall be necessary and proper for carrying into execution the foregoing powers, and all other powers vested by this Constitution in the Government of the United States, or in any department or officer thereof.

Sec. 9. The migration or importation of such persons as any of the States now existing shall think proper to admit, shall not be prohibited by the Congress prior to the year one thousand eight hundred and eight, but a tax or duty may be imposed on such importation, not exceeding ten dollars for each person.

The privilege of the writ of habeas corpus shall not be suspended, unless when in cases of rebellion or invasion the public safety may require it.

No bill of attainder or ex post facto law shall be passed.

No capitation, or other direct, tax shall be laid, unless in proportion to the census or enumeration herein before directed to be taken.

No tax or duty shall be laid on articles exported from any State.

No preference shall be given by any regulation of commerce or revenue to the ports of one State over those of another: nor shall vessels bound to, or from, one State, be obliged to enter, clear, or pay duties in another.

No money shall be drawn from the Treasury but in consequence of appropriations made by law; and a regular statement and account of the receipts and expenditures of all public money shall be published from time to time.

No title of nobility shall be granted by the United States: and no person holding any office of profit or trust under them, shall, without the consent of the Congress, accept of any present, emolument, office, or title, of any kind whatever, from any king, prince or foreign State.

Sec. 10. No State shall enter into any treaty, alliance, or confederation; grant letters of marque and reprisal; coin money; emit bills of credit; make any thing but gold and silver coin a tender in payment of debts; pass any bill of attainder, ex post facto law, or law impairing the obligation of contracts, or grant any title of nobility.

No State shall, without the consent of the Congress, lay any imposts or duties on imports or exports, except what may be absolutely necessary for executing its inspection laws: and the net produce of all duties and imposts, laid by any State on imports or exports, shall be for the use of the Treasury of the United States; and all such laws shall be subject to the revision and control of the Congress.

No State shall, without the consent of Congress, lay any duty of tonnage, keep troops, or ships of war in time of peace, enter into any agreement or compact with another State, or with a foreign power, or engage in war, unless actually invaded, or in such imminent danger as will not admit of delay.

Article II

Sec. 1. The executive power shall be vested in a President of the United States of America. He shall hold his office during the term of four years, and, together with the Vice-President, chosen for the same term, be elected, as follows:

Each State shall appoint, in such manner as the legislature thereof may direct, a number of electors, equal to the whole number of Senators and Representatives to which the State may be entitled in the Congress: but no Senator or Representative, or person holding an office of trust or profit under the United States, shall be appointed an elector.

The electors shall meet in their respective States, and vote by ballot for two persons, of whom one at least shall not be an inhabitant of the same State with themselves. And they shall make a list of all the persons voted for, and of the number of votes for each; which list they shall sign and certify, and transmit sealed to the seat of the Government of the United States, directed to the President of the Senate. The President of the Senate shall, in the presence of the Senate and House of Representatives, open all the certificates, and the votes shall then be counted. The person having the greatest number of votes shall be the President, if such number be a majority of the whole number of electors appointed; and if there be more than one who have such majority, and have an equal number of votes, then the House of Representatives shall immediately choose by ballot one of them for President; and if no person have a majority, then from the five highest on the list the said house shall in like manner choose the President. But in choosing the President, the votes shall be taken by States, the representation from each State having one vote; a quorum for this purpose shall consist of a member or members from two-thirds of the States, and a majority of all the States shall be necessary to a choice. In every case, after the choice of the President, the person having the greatest number of votes of the electors shall be the Vice-President. But if there should remain two or more who have equal votes, the Senate shall choose from them by ballot the Vice-President.

The Congress may determine the time of choosing the electors, and the day on which they shall give their votes; which day shall be the same throughout the United States.

No person except a natural-born citizen, or a citizen of the United States, at the time of the adoption of this Constitution, shall be eligible to the office of President; neither shall any person be eligible to that office who shall not have attained to the age of thirty-five years, and been fourteen years a resident within the United States.

In case of the removal of the President from office, or of his death, resignation, or inability to discharge the powers and duties of the said office, the same shall devolve on the Vice-President, and the Congress may by law provide for the case of removal, death, resignation, or inability, both of the President and Vice-President, declaring what officer shall then act as President, and such officer shall act accordingly, until the disability be removed, or a President shall be elected.

The President shall, at stated times, receive for his services, a compensation, which shall neither be increased nor diminished during the period for which he shall have been elected, and he shall not receive within that period any other emolument from the United States, or any of them.

Before he enter on the execution of his office, he shall take the following oath or affirmation: 'I do solemnly swear (or affirm) that I will faithfully execute the office of President of the United States, and will to the best of my ability, preserve, protect, and defend the Constitution of the United States.'

Sec. 2. The President shall be Commander-in-Chief of the Army and Navy of the United States, and of the militia of the several States, when called into the actual service of the United States; he may require the opinion, in writing, of the principal officer in each of the executive departments, upon any subject relating to the duties of their respective offices, and he shall have power to grant reprieves and pardons for offences against the United States, except in cases of impeachment.

He shall have power, by and with the advice and consent of the Senate, to make treaties, provided two-thirds of the Senators present concur; and he shall nominate, and by and with the advice and consent of the Senate, shall appoint ambassadors, other public ministers and consuls, judges of the Supreme Court, and all other officers of the United States, whose appointments are not herein otherwise provided for, and which shall be established by law: but the Congress may by law vest the appointment of such inferior officers, as they think proper, in the President alone, in the courts of law, or in the heads of departments.

The President shall have power to fill up all vacancies that may happen during the recess of the Senate, by granting commissions which shall expire at the end of their next session.

Sec. 3. He shall from time to time give to the Congress information of the state of the Union, and recommend to their consideration such measures as he shall judge necessary and expedient; he may, on extraordinary occasions, convene both houses, or either of them, and in case of disagreement between them, with respect to the time of adjournment, he may adjourn them to such time as he shall think proper; he shall receive ambassadors and other public ministers; he shall take care that the laws be faithfully executed, and shall commission all the officers of the United States.

Sec. 4. The President, Vice-President and all civil officers of the United States, shall be removed from office on impeachment for, and conviction of, treason, bribery, or other high crimes and misdemeanors.

ARTICLE III

Sec. 1. The judicial power of the United States, shall be vested in one Supreme Court, and in such inferior courts as the Congress may from time to time ordain and establish. The judges, both of the supreme and inferior courts, shall hold their offices during good behaviour, and shall, at stated times, receive for their services, a compensation, which shall not be diminished during their continuance in office.

Sec. 2. The judicial power shall extend to all cases, in law and equity, arising under this Constitution, the laws of the United States, and treaties made, or which shall be made, under their authority; to all cases affecting ambassadors, other public ministers and consuls; to all cases of admiralty and maritime jurisdiction; to controversies to which the United States shall be a party; to controversies between two or more States; between a State and citizens of another State; between citizens of different States, between citizens of the same State claiming lands under grants of different States, and between a State, or the citizens thereof, and foreign States, citizens or subjects.

In all cases affecting ambassadors, other public ministers and consuls, and those in which a State shall be party, the Supreme Court shall have original jurisdiction. In all the other cases before mentioned, the Supreme Court shall have appellate jurisdiction, both as to law and fact, with such exceptions, and under such regulations as the Congress shall make.

The trial of all crimes, except in cases of impeachment, shall be by jury; and such trial shall be held in the State where the said crimes shall have been committed; but when not committed within any State, the trial shall be at such place or places as the Congress may by law have directed.

Sec. 3. Treason against the United States, shall consist only in levying war against them, or in adhering to their enemies, giving them aid and comfort. No person shall be convicted of treason unless on the testimony of two witnesses to the same overt act, or on confession in open court.

The Congress shall have power to declare the punishment of treason, but no attainder of treason shall work corruption of blood, or forfeiture except during the life of the person attainted.

ARTICLE IV

Sec. 1. Full faith and credit shall be given in each State to the public acts, records, and judicial proceedings of every other State. And the Congress may by general laws prescribe the manner in which such acts, records, and proceedings shall be provided, and the effect thereof.

Sec. 2. The citizens of each State shall be entitled to all privileges and immunities of citizens in the several States.

A person charged in any State with treason, felony, or other crime, who shall flee from justice, and be found in another State, shall on demand of the executive authority of the State from which he fled, be delivered up, to be removed to the State having jurisdiction of the crime.

No person held to service or labor in one State, under the laws thereof, escaping into another, shall, in consequence of any law or regulation therein, be discharged from such service or labor, but shall be delivered up on claim of the party to whom such service or labor may be due.

Sec. 3. New States may be admitted by the Congress into this Union; but no new States shall be formed or erected within the jurisdiction of any other State; nor any State be formed by the junction of two or more states; or parts of States, without the consent of the legislatures of the States concerned as well as of the Congress.

The Congress shall have power to dispose of and make all needful rules and regulations respecting the territory or other property belonging to the United States; and nothing in this Constitution shall be so construed as to prejudice any claims of the United States, or of any particular State.

Sec. 4. The United States shall guarantee to every State in this Union a republican form of government, and shall protect each of them against invasion; and on application of the legislature, or of the executive (when the legislature cannot be convened) against domestic violence.

ARTICLE V

The Congress, whenever two-thirds of both houses shall deem it necessary, shall propose amendments to this Constitution, or, on the application of the legislatures of two-thirds of the several States, shall call a convention for proposing amendments, which, in either case, shall be valid to all intents and purposes, as part of this Constitution, when ratified by the legislatures of three-fourths of the several States, or by conventions in three-fourths thereof, as the one or the other mode of ratification may be proposed by the Congress; provided that no amendment which may be made prior to the year one thousand eight hundred and eight shall in any manner affect the first and fourth clauses in the ninth section of the first article; and that no State, without its consent, shall be deprived of its equal suffrage in the Senate.

ARTICLE VI

All debts contracted and engagements entered into, before the adoption of this Constitution, shall be as valid against the United States under this Constitution, as under the Confederation.

This Constitution, and the laws of the United States which shall be made in pursuance thereof; and all treaties made, or which shall be made, under the authority of the United States, shall be the supreme law of the land; and the judges in every State shall be bound thereby, anything in the Constitution or laws of any State to the contrary notwithstanding.

The Senators and Representatives before mentioned, and the members of the several State legislatures, and all executive and judicial officers, both of the United States and of the several States, shall be bound by oath or affirmation, to support this Constitution; but no religious test shall ever be required as a qualification to any office or public trust under the United States.

ARTICLE VII

The ratification of the conventions of nine States, shall be sufficient for the establishment of this Constitution between the States so ratifying the same.

Done in convention by the unanimous consent of the States present, the seventeenth day of September in the year of our Lord one thousand seven hundred and eighty-seven and of the independence of the United States of America the twelfth. In witness whereof, we have hereunto subscribed our names,

G° WASHINGTON—Presid^t and deputy from Virginia

New Hampshire
JOHN LANGDON
NICHOLAS GILMAN
Massachusetts
NATHANIEL GORHAM
RUFUS KING
Connecticut
W^M SAM^L JOHNSON
ROGER SHERMAN
New York
ALEXANDER HAMILTON
New Jersey
WIL: LIVINGSTON
DAVID BREARLEY
W^M PATERSON
JONA: DAYTON
Pennsylvania
B. FRANKLIN
THOMAS MIFFLIN
ROB^T MORRIS
GEO. CLYMER
THO^S FITZSIMONS
JARED INGERSOLL
JAMES WILSON
GOUV MORRIS

Delaware
GEO: READ
GUNNING BEDFORD jun
JOHN DICKINSON
RICHARD BASSETT
JACO: BROOM
Maryland
JAMES M^{C}HENRY
DAN OF S^T THO^S JENIFER
DAN^L CARROLL
Virginia
JOHN BLAIR
JAMES MADISON JR.
North Carolina
W^M BLOUNT
RICH^D DOBBS SPAIGHT
HU WILLIAMSON
South Carolina
J. RUTLEDGE
CHARLES COTESWORTH
  PINCKNEY
CHARLES PINCKNEY
PIERCE BUTLER
Georgia
WILLIAM FEW
ABR BALDWIN

Amendments to the Constitution

ARTICLES I-X (the Bill of Rights) 1791.

ARTICLE I

Congress shall make no law respecting an establishment of religion, or prohibiting the free exercise thereof; or abridging the freedom of speech, or of the press; or the right of the people peaceably to assemble, and to petition the government for a redress of grievances.

ARTICLE II

A well regulated militia, being necessary to the security of a free State, the right of the people to keep and bear arms, shall not be infringed.

ARTICLE III

No soldier shall, in time of peace be quartered in any house, without the consent of the owner, nor in time of war, but in a manner to be prescribed by law.

ARTICLE IV

The right of the people to be secure in their persons, houses, papers, and effects, against unreasonable searches and seizures, shall not be violated, and no warrants shall issue, but upon probable cause, supported by oath or affirmation, and particularly describing the place to be searched, and the persons or things to be seized.

ARTICLE V

No person shall be held to answer for a capital, or otherwise infamous crime, unless on a presentment or indictment of a grand jury, except in cases arising in the land or naval forces, or in the militia, when in actual service in time of war or public danger; nor shall any person be subject for the same offence to be twice put in jeopardy of life or limb; nor shall be compelled in any criminal case to be a witness against himself, nor be deprived of life, liberty, or property, without due process of law; nor shall private property be taken for public use, without just compensation.

ARTICLE VI

In all criminal prosecutions, the accused shall enjoy the right to a speedy and public trial, by an impartial jury of the State and district wherein the crime shall have been committed, which district shall have been previously ascertained by law, and to be informed of the nature and cause of the accusation; to be confronted with the witnesses against him; to have compulsory process for obtaining witnesses in his favor, and to have the assistance of counsel for his defence.

ARTICLE VII

In suits at common law, where the value in controversy shall exceed twenty dollars, the right of trial by jury shall be preserved, and no fact tried by a jury, shall be otherwise re-examined in any court of the United States, than according to the rules of the common law.

ARTICLE VIII

Excessive bail shall not be required, nor excessive fines imposed, nor cruel and unusual punishments inflicted.

ARTICLE IX

The enumeration in the Constitution, of certain rights, shall not be construed to deny or disparage others retained by the people.

ARTICLE X

The powers not delegated to the United States by the Constitution, nor prohibited by it to the States, are reserved to the States respectively, or to the people.

ARTICLE XI (1798)

The judicial power of the United States shall not be construed to extend to any suit in law or equity, commenced or prosecuted against one of the United States by citizens of another State, or by citizens or subjects of any foreign State.

ARTICLE XII (1804)

The electors shall meet in their respective states, and vote by ballot for President and Vice-President, one of whom at least, shall not be an inhabitant of the same state with themselves; they shall name in their ballots the person voted for as President, and in distinct ballots the person voted for as Vice-President, and they shall make distinct lists of all persons voted for as President, and of all persons voted for as Vice-President, and of the number of votes for each, which lists they shall sign and certify, and transmit sealed to the seat of the Government of the United States, directed to the President of the Senate; The President of the Senate shall, in the presence of the Senate and House of Representatives, open all the certificates and the votes shall then be counted; The person having the greatest number of votes for President, shall be the President, if such number be a majority of the whole number of electors appointed; and if no person have such majority, then from the persons having the highest numbers not exceeding three on the list of those voted for as President, the House of Representatives shall choose immediately, by ballot, the President. But in choosing the President, the votes shall be taken by states, the representation from each state having one vote; a quorum for this purpose shall consist of a member or members from two-thirds of the states, and a majority of all the states shall be necessary to a choice. And if the House of

Representatives shall not choose a President whenever the right of choice shall devolve upon them, before the fourth day of March next following, then the Vice-President shall act as President, as in the case of death or other constitutional disability of the President. The person having the greatest number of votes as Vice-President, shall be the Vice-President, if such number be a majority of the whole number of electors appointed, and if no person have a majority, then from the two highest numbers on the list, the Senate shall choose the Vice-President; a quorum for the purpose shall consist of two-thirds of the whole number of Senators, and a majority of the whole number shall be necessary to a choice. But no person constitutionally ineligible to the office of President shall be eligible to that of Vice-President of the United States.

Article XIII (1865)

Sec. 1. Neither slavery nor involuntary servitude, except as a punishment for crime whereof the party shall have been duly convicted, shall exist within the United States, or any place subject to their jurisdiction.

Sec. 2. Congress shall have power to enforce this article by appropriate legislation.

Article XIV (1868)

Sec. 1. All persons born or naturalized in the United States, and subject to the jurisdiction thereof, are citizens of the United States and of the State wherein they reside. No State shall make or enforce any law which shall abridge the privileges or immunities of citizens of the United States; nor shall any State deprive any person of life, liberty, or property, without due process of law; nor deny to any person within its jurisdiction the equal protection of the laws.

Sec. 2. Representatives shall be appointed among the several States according to their respective numbers, counting the whole number of persons in each State, excluding Indians not taxed. But when the right to vote at any election for the choice of electors for President and Vice-President of the United

States, Representatives in Congress, the executive and judicial officers of a State, or the members of the legislature thereof, is denied to any of the male inhabitants of such State, being twenty-one years of age, and citizens of the United States, or in any way abridged, except for participation in rebellion, or other crime, the basis of representation therein shall be reduced in the proportion which the number of such male citizens shall bear to the whole number of male citizens twenty-one years of age in such State.

Sec. 3. No person shall be a Senator or Representative in Congress, or elector of President and Vice-President, or hold any office, civil or military, under the United States, or under any State, who, having previously taken an oath, as a member of Congress, or as an officer of the United States, or as a member of any State legislature, or as an executive or judicial officer of any State; to support the Constitution of the United States, shall have engaged in insurrection or rebellion against the same, or given aid or comfort to the enemies thereof. But Congress may by a vote of two-thirds of each house, remove such disability.

Sec. 4. The validity of the public debt of the United States, authorized by law, including debts incurred for payment of pensions and bounties for services in suppressing insurrection or rebellion, shall not be questioned. But neither the United States nor any State shall assume or pay any debt or obligation incurred in aid of insurrection or rebellion against the United States, or any claim for the loss or emancipation of any slave; but all such debts, obligations and claims shall be held illegal and void.

Sec. 5. The Congress shall have power to enforce, by appropriate legislation, the provisions of this article.

ARTICLE XV (1870)

Sec. 1. The right of citizens of the United States to vote shall not be denied or abridged by the United States or by any State on account of race, color, or previous condition of servitude.

Sec. 2. The Congress shall have power to enforce this article by appropriate legislation.

ARTICLE XVI (1913)

The Congress shall have power to lay and collect taxes on incomes, from whatever source derived, without apportionment among the several States and without regard to any census or enumeration.

ARTICLE XVII (1913)

The Senate of the United States shall be composed of two Senators from each State, elected by the people thereof, for six years; and each Senator shall have one vote. The electors in each State shall have the qualifications requisite for electors of the most numerous branch of the State legislature.

When vacancies happen in the representation of any State in the Senate, the executive authority of such State shall issue writs of election to fill such vacancies: *Provided,* That the legislature of any State may empower the executive thereof to make temporary appointments until the people fill the vacancies by election as the legislature may direct.

This amendment shall not be so construed as to affect the election or term of any Senator chosen before it becomes valid as part of the Constitution.

ARTICLE XVIII (1919)

After one year from the ratification of this article, the manufacture, sale, or transportation of intoxicating liquors within, the importation thereof into, or the exportation thereof from the United States and all territory subject to the jurisdiction thereof for beverage purposes is hereby prohibited.

The Congress and the several States shall have concurrent power to enforce this article by appropriate legislation.

This article shall be inoperative unless it shall have been ratified as an amendment to the Constitution by the legislatures of the several States, as provided in the Constitution, within seven years from the date of the submission hereof to the States by Congress.

ARTICLE XIX (1920)

The right of citizens of the United States to vote shall not be denied or abridged by the United States or by any States on account of sex.

The Congress shall have power by appropriate legislation to enforce the provisions of this article.

ARTICLE XX (1933)

Sec. 1. The terms of the President and Vice-President shall end at noon on the twentieth day of January, and the terms of Senators and Representatives at noon on the third day of January, of the years in which such terms would have ended if this article had not been ratified; and the terms of their successors shall then begin.

Sec. 2. The Congress shall assemble at least once in every year, and such meeting shall begin at noon on the third day of January, unless they shall by law appoint a different day.

Sec. 3. If, at the time fixed for the beginning of the term of the President, the President-elect shall have died, the Vice-President-elect shall become President. If a President shall not have been chosen before the time fixed for the beginning of his term, or if the President-elect shall have failed to qualify, then the Vice-President-elect shall act as President until a President shall have qualified; and the Congress may by law provide for the case wherein neither a President-elect nor a Vice-President-elect shall have qualified, declaring who shall then act as President, or the manner in which one who is to act shall be selected, and such person shall act accordingly until a President or Vice-President shall have qualified.

Sec. 4. The Congress may by law provide for the case of the death of any of the persons from whom the House of Representatives may choose a President whenever the right of choice shall have devolved upon them, and for the case of the death of any of the persons from whom the Senate may choose a

Vice-President whenever the right of choice shall have devolved upon them.

Sec. 5. Sections 1 and 2 shall take effect on the Fifteenth day of October following the ratification of this article.

Sec. 6. This article shall be inoperative unless it shall have been ratified as an amendment to the Constitution by the legislatures of three-fourths of the several States within seven years from the date of its submission.

ARTICLE XXI (1933)

Sec. 1. The eighteenth article of amendment to the Constitution of the United States is hereby repealed.

Sec. 2. The transportation or importation into any State, territory or possession of the United States for delivery or use therein of intoxicating liquors, in violation of the laws thereof, is hereby prohibited.

Sec. 3. This article shall be inoperative unless it shall have been ratified as an amendment to the Constitution by convention in the several States, as provided in the Constitution, within seven years from the date of the submission thereof to the States by the Congress.

ARTICLE XXII (1951)

Sec. 1. No person shall be elected to the office of the President more than twice, and no person who has held the office of President, or acted as President, for more than two years of a term to which some other person was elected President shall be elected to the office of the President more than once. But this Article shall not apply to any person holding the office of President when this Article was proposed by the Congress, and shall not prevent any person who may be holding the office of President, or acting as President, during the term within which this Article becomes operative, from holding the office of President or acting as President during the remainder of such term.

Sec. 2. This article shall be inoperative unless it shall have been ratified as an amendment to the Constitution by the legislatures of three-fourths of the several States within seven years from the date of its submission to the States by the Congress.

Article XXIII (1961)

Sec. 1. The District constituting the seat of Government of the United States shall appoint in such manner as Congress may direct:

A number of electors of President and Vice-President equal to the whole number of Senators and Representatives in Congress to which the District would be entitled if it were a state, but in no event more than the least populous state; they shall be in addition to those appointed by the States, but they shall be considered, for the purposes of the election of President and Vice-President, to be electors appointed by a State; and they shall meet in the District and perform such duties as provided by the twelfth article of amendment.

Sec. 2. The Congress shall have power to enforce this article by appropriate legislation.

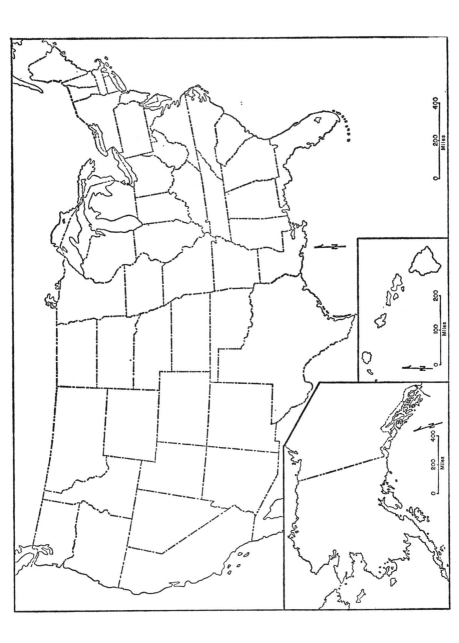

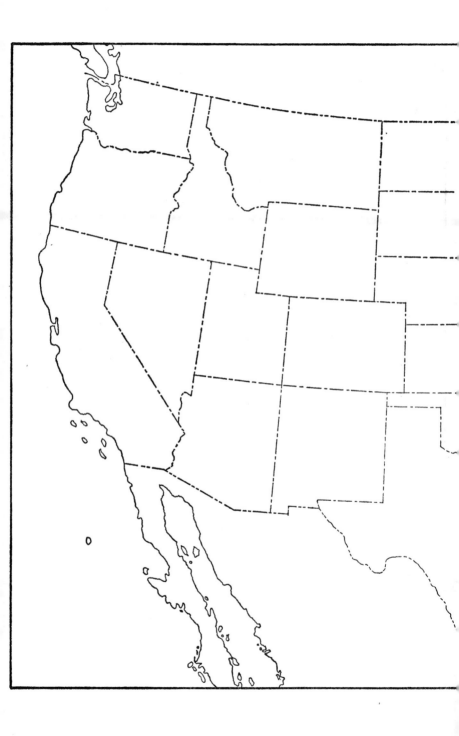

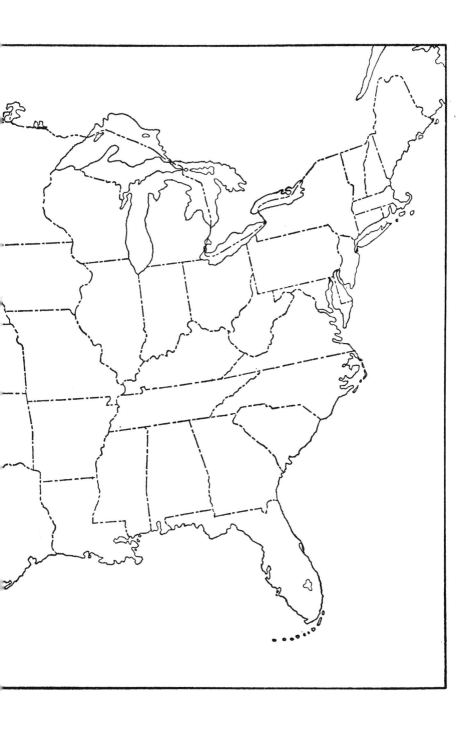

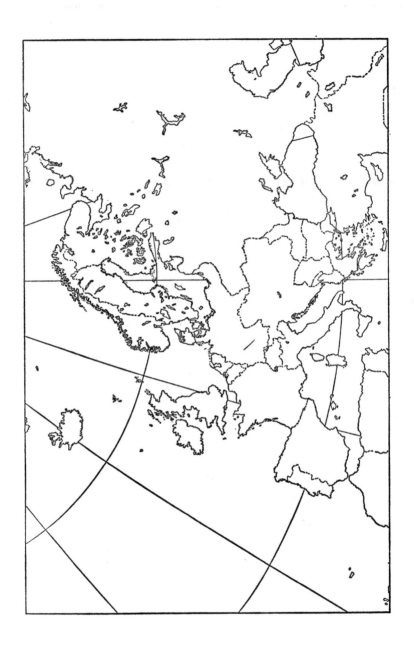